V

CASE STUDIES IN MACROECONOMICS

Economics Association Teaching Materials Project

CASE STUDIES IN ECONOMIC ANALYSIS

Series Editor : W. Peter J. Maunder

A series of detailed case studies designed to
enhance an understanding of real-world issues
for the student taking a degree course, professional
examination or Advanced level G.C.E. in Economics

1. *Case Studies in Competition Policy,* by Keith J. Blois, W. Stewart Howe and W. Peter J. Maunder
2. *Case Studies in Cost-Benefit Analysis,* by Kenneth J. Button and Peter J. Barker
3. *Case Studies in Regional Economics,* by Kenneth J. Button and D. Gillingwater
4. *Case Studies in the Competitive Process,* by Peter J. Barker, Keith J. Blois, W. Stewart Howe, W. Peter J. Maunder and Michael J. Tighe
5. *Case Studies in Macroeconomics,* edited by W. Peter J. Maunder
6. *Case Studies in International Economics,* edited by W. Peter J. Maunder

CASE STUDIES IN ECONOMIC ANALYSIS

V

CASE STUDIES IN MACROECONOMICS

Edited by
Peter Maunder

*Department of Economics,
Loughborough University*

**John Day
Jim Hough
Gavin Kennedy
Peter Maunder
Chris Milner
Michael Parr
John Presley
Michael Tighe**

Published by Heinemann Educational Books
on behalf of the Economics Association

Heinemann Educational Books Ltd

LONDON   EDINBURGH   MELBOURNE   AUCKLAND   TORONTO
HONG KONG   SINGAPORE   KUALA LUMPUR   NEW DELHI
NAIROBI   JOHANNESBURG   LUSAKA   IBADAN   KINGSTON

Students' edition ISBN 0 435 84473 3
Teacher's Guide ISBN 0 435 84474 1

First published 1977

Published by Heinemann Educational Books Ltd
48 Charles Street, London W1X 8AH
Printed in Great Britain by
Cox & Wyman Ltd
London, Fakenham and Reading

Contents

In the *Teacher's Guide* only, Teacher's Notes begin on page 90

Introduction

This is the fifth text in the *Case Studies in Economic Analysis* series but is the first one to deal with macroeconomic issues. Microeconomics of its very nature lends itself more readily to the case study approach than does the study of the determination and inter-relationship between national income aggregates. It is indeed a moot point whether issues such as those examined in this text are topics or themes rather than case studies. Whatever the view on this point this text focuses on some very relevant problems concerning the British economy.

In the first study Jim Hough considers the problem of financing the United Kingdom public sector. The current attention given to the size of this sector's deficit in the mid-1970s is put into context in considering the growth of the National Debt.

Gavin Kennedy's case study explores an important area of public policy: whether Scotland is economically viable as an independent country. This study was chosen to illustrate a basic part of any macro course – the measurement of gross national product of a country. In this case study it is shown that there has been a fascinating change in the nature of the debate concerning Scotland in economic terms.

In the third study Michael Tighe has examined the level and composition of savings, particularly personal savings, using material provided and researched by Peter Maunder. It shows that the sluggish nature of savings in the 1960s has given way to an unexpected rise in the 1970s. Macroeconomics courses never fail to consider the nature of consumption expenditures. This case study examines the neglected aspect – that part of incomes which is not currently spent.

Michael Parr and John Day offer a fourth case study concerned with the rationale of introducing V.A.T. in the UK and its effects in practice. The readily available literature on this recent addition to the government's fiscal powers is remarkably small and the case study is a welcome appraisal of this tax.

The final case study offers an international comparison of the growth and stability aspects of the macroeconomic system. John Presley and Christopher Milner compare the progress of the UK and West German economies and offer a wider perspective than the usual diagnosis of Britain's economic ills.

The case studies are structured in four parts. Firstly, there is the material in the case study. Then follow about a dozen questions requiring the student to think about the facts and issues contained in the case study. In the Teacher's Guide there are some suggested 'answers' to these questions. It is stressed that the questions may lead to students offering alternative conclusions and analyses to those in this section, which may be quite legitimate in the light of the information in the case study. The answers are thus not intended to be exhaustive but are considered the major 'Points intended to be raised from the questions'. This section is headed as in this quotation rather than 'Answers' to avoid misconceptions on this score. The Teacher's Guide also provides information on the case studies. The intention here is in part to give the teacher an up-to-date picture of the situation in case students ask about this, and also to give him further material for class use if he wishes. Not all case study books offer 'answers' to qualitative questions and few give notes bringing the teacher right up to date. These studies offer *both* these aids.

The diagnostic powers required for using these studies are those possessed by capable Advanced level students. It is hoped the book will appeal to those teaching either a first-year degree course in Economics or one in Macroeconomics.

Each of the studies can be read by the students prior to class discussion of the questions or alternatively begun from scratch. In the latter case a double lesson, typical of Sixth Form teaching, should be found adequate to cover one case. The studies can of course be set to students individually and written rather than oral answers sought.

The United Kingdom's Public Sector Debt

HISTORICAL BACKGROUND

'Budget deficit', 'national debt', 'public sector borrowing requirement' and similar phrases constantly recur in the national press and indicate that the topic considered in this case study, the indebtedness of the government machine, seems to be frequently in the news. In his 'budget' of December 1976 the Chancellor of the Exchequer, Dennis Healey, said he was hoping to reduce the central government's budget deficit to some £8,600 million by the end of the 1978–79 financial year.[1]

Table 1.1 Growth of the National Debt

	(£m.)
1694	1
1800	200
1815	800
1914	650
1918	8,000
1939	8,600
1945	26,000
1966	31,000
1976	54,041

Source: (For 1976) 'Distribution of the national debt at end-March 1976', *Bank of England Quarterly Bulletin*, Vol. 16, No. 4, December 1976, p. 447. The definition used is 'the total of liabilities in sterling of the National Loans Fund together with nationalised industries' stocks guaranteed by the Government'.

All this would have been inconceivable to virtually any economist before the late 1930s: the attitude of the 'classical economists' to the government's budget was quite clear and was not even considered to be a matter for discussion. Only during war-time was it permissible for the government to borrow, i.e. to run a budget deficit; during years of peace (i.e. throughout the period 1815–1914, save for the short and relatively minor Crimean and Boer Wars), the government had to balance its books, matching expenditure to income. This 'Gladstonian finance' could be parsimonious in its implications for government spending and at times caused headaches for the government of the day: Gladstone himself, for example, when he reluctantly agreed to send the small British force into Egypt in 1882 (the start of the 'Scramble for Africa' by the European powers) was worried over the additional taxes he had to raise to meet this new expenditure. Table 1.1 shows that the attitude that the government should only incur debt during a major war was adhered to right down to 1945.

This table also makes it apparent that a major change in attitude must have occurred around 1945 because subsequently the Debt has continued to increase steadily at an average rate of about £900 million per year. Before we discuss the reasons for this, however, we must pause to consider the nature of these statistics.

Theoretically we should be interested in all borrowing on the part of the government sector of the economy or, as one definition puts it, 'the total net indebtedness of the public sector to the private sector', and we must bear in mind that 'the public sector' includes both local government authorities and nationalized industries in addition to the central government. The Bank of England's official statistics for the 'National Debt', however, not only relate mainly to the central government but they also include stocks and other assets held temporarily for some reason by governmental bodies.[2] On balance they grossly *underestimate* the total debt of the public sector. Therefore, in order to arrive at an approximate estimate of the total debt of the public sector, we need to take the 'National Debt', *add* on those debts of local authorities and nationalized industries not already included, but then *deduct* those stocks held within the public sector. The 1975 'Annual Abstract of Statistics' does a partial exercise on these lines but by further adaptation we can arrive at the estimate given in Table 1.2, and even this estimate is inaccurate since it ignores the double-counting represented by the borrowing from the central

Table 1.2 The Total Debt of the Public Sector as at March 1974

	(£m.)
The National Debt	40,125
Local authorities' gross debt	22,740
Public corporations' gross debt	16,361
Notes and Coin in circulation	5,082
Miscellaneous	4,149
Gross Total	88,457
Less: held within the public sector (estimated)	35,759
Estimated total public sector debt	52,698

N.B. Notes and Coin in circulation are not, of course, debt in the same sense as used elsewhere in this case study but technically they do represent obligations of the central government.

Source: Estimates based on Bank of England data.

government by the public corporations (£13,560 million) and the local authorities (£9,488 million).

We therefore find that the total debt of the public sector is a colossal sum: at about 70 per cent of our Gross National Product, it represents a far higher relative burden than that of any other major developed country. When our 'National debt excluding official holdings' amounted to 42 per cent of GNP in 1973/74, no other comparable country had a figure exceeding 22 per cent (USA and Canada), whilst those of West Germany and Italy (11 per cent) or France (7 per cent) were far lower.

We can now consider why attitudes towards the incurring of government debt changed significantly at around the end of World War II and this inevitably involves the name of John Maynard Keynes. Keynes' *General Theory* was published in 1936 and its essential policy message was endorsed in the Chancellor's budget speech in 1941 and specifically accepted as government policy in the 1944 White Paper on Employment. In summary, this message was that the economy would not normally settle down at the level of activity which would generate full employment and that the government therefore had a duty to intervene to regulate the level of aggregate demand. In particular, during a period of high unemployment, such as Britain had experienced in the 1930s, the government should increase public expenditure and/or reduce taxation in order to achieve an increase in the level of economic activity: the ensuing multiplier effects would lead to a cumulative process of job creation. 'Keynesian economics' developed gradually in the years after Keynes' death until the Radcliffe Report, published in 1959, could refer to the complex and sometimes conflicting aims of macroeconomic policy as:[3]

1. the avoidance of inflation;
2. the maintenance of full employment;
3. the achievement of a balance-of-payments equilibrium and stability of the external value of sterling;
4. the fostering of economic growth;
5. and even aiding the developing countries.

The 'management' of the economy, or 'fine-tuning' as it has been called, in pursuit of these aims, has been perhaps the major preoccupation of the government of the day throughout the whole of the post-war period.[4] From the point of view of this case study, it should be clear that, once there is a commitment to take such steps as increasing public expenditure or decreasing taxation for macroeconomic policy purposes, it is no longer possible to adhere to the view of the classical economists regarding a balanced budget and no additional debt. A budget deficit, and therefore an increase in the government's debt may result, and in fact throughout the years 1945 to 1977 the central government has had an overall budget deficit in every year except two, 1969 and 1970. When we add to this the prodigious regular borrowing by local authorities since the mid-1950s and the more spasmodic and irregular deficits incurred by the nationalized industries, we have a picture of the total public sector debt growing constantly and at an ever-increasing rate. It should be understood that all this stems from the Keynesian revolution in economic thought; one only has to look at a country which has never accepted a Keynesian-type approach, such as France, to find that the government's approach to fiscal policy still centres on achieving a balanced budget each year.[5]

TRENDS OVER TIME

At this point the reader may be coming to the conclusion that the picture of Britain's public sector sinking further and further into debt is rather worrying. To examine this proposition, let us now examine the figures rather more closely: taking a ten-year movement from 1963 to 1973 should give an indication of trends over time (the figures for 1974, 1975 and 1976 reveal certain quite distinct new characteristics and will therefore be considered separately later).

Table 1.3 Deficit financing, 1963 and 1973 (£m.)

	1963	1973
Central government:		
Current account surplus	240	1,001
Plus: Taxes on capital	308	823
'Corrected' surplus	548	1,824
Extra borrowing on Capital account[a] (= national debt increase)	153	2,341
Total capital expenditure	2,265	4,081

[a]After allowing for various other receipts.
Source: *National Income and Expenditure Blue Book*, annually from H.M.S.O.

As Table 1.3 indicates, the central government made a healthy surplus on its current account (i.e. after having used the proceeds of taxation to pay all current items such as wages and salaries, lighting and heating, current supplies, etc.). The official statistics for the current account surplus, however, are misleading since capital taxes are not included but are shown separately in the capital account. Whilst this seems logical to an accountant, to an economist it is nonsensical: capital taxes have a similar economic function to other taxes and have no direct relation to the government's capital expenditure. Therefore we need to add them back on in order to arrive at a 'corrected' surplus. It can now be seen that the current surplus is devoted to capital account purposes (building of motorways, hospitals, schools, etc.) and that in the years in question about one-quarter to one-half of such capital expenditure was paid for out of current taxation, the remainder, after certain miscellaneous receipts, being borrowed. Whilst there were obviously fluctuations from year to year, for the thirty-year period up to 1974 these figures are fairly typical: they indicate that the extra debt is more than offset by the acquisition of capital of various kinds. In order to know, however, whether the country's 'worth' (as measured by the net increase in public capital) was increasing more rapidly than the debt, we should need to know the total annual depreciation on all government property and other capital: the *National Income and Expenditure Blue Book* estimates capital consumption by the central government at £279 million for 1975 (£166 million for 1973), but these can be no more than approximate estimations: on that basis, the net increase in capital values certainly exceeds the increase in the National Debt.

We can now look at the relationship between the increase in the National Debt and other key indicators in the economy.

Table 1.4 Relative Position of National Debt

	1963	1973
National Debt (March)	£29,807m.	£36,526m.
Gross National Product	£27,279m.	£64,830m.
National Debt as % of GNP	110%	56%
Interest payments on the Debt[a]	£930m.	£1,762m.
Interest payments as % of GNP	3·4%	2·7%
Interest payments as % of total central government current expenditure	11·57%	8·29%

[a] These interest payments are gross and are eventually offset by receipts from local authorities and nationalized industries.

Source: *National Income and Expenditure Blue Books.*

We see from Table 1.4 that, although the increase in the National Debt over this period looks very large in monetary terms (it would, of course, look much smaller if the figures were deflated to give 'real' values, i.e. to remove the effects of price changes), it is smaller than the rise in Gross National Product and the Debt as a percentage of GNP has declined markedly. Similarly, the annual interest payments on the Debt have, in spite of the trend towards higher interest rates over these years, become smaller in relation to either GNP or to total central government current expenditure. We may therefore make an analogy with a man who has acquired a larger mortgage on his house but whose annual income has risen proportionately more than either the amount of the mortgage or the annual payments he has to make to the building society. Once viewed in this light, the debt seems much less worrying and some of the fears hinted at above can in fact be allayed.

RECENT CHANGES

Unfortunately, however, the picture changes again when we look at the most recent figures, as outlined in Table 1.5.

Table 1.5 Central Government Accounts, 1974–75 (£m.)

	1974	1975
Central government:		
Current account surplus	310	−1,397
Plus: Taxes on capital	860	828
'Corrected' surplus	1,170	−569
Total capital expenditure	5,301	6,971
Increase in national debt	3,538	8,381

Source: *National Income and Expenditure Blue Books.*

It immediately becomes apparent that a significant change has occurred although this should not be seen as a sudden or dramatic switch: the current account surplus has in fact been diminishing, and the borrowing requirement increasing, steadily since 1970. By 1974 we see that the uncorrected surplus had fallen dangerously low (and to less than one-tenth of its 1970 value in monetary terms) and the corrected surplus was able to finance only about one-fifth of capital expenditure. By 1975 there was actually a deficit on the current account and the increased debt exceeded the total capital expenditure. This means that the government was borrowing in order to pay for items of *current* expenditure, which is a situation that has probably never previously occurred in this country in peacetime. It is, in fact, difficult to exaggerate the seriousness of such a situation: not only was the additional debt extremely large (more than double 1974's record figure) but it was in no sense matched by the acquisition of capital items, which has always been the case previously. Our previous analogy must now be amended to that of a man who takes out an additional mortgage in order to pay for his current central heating bill, or for his wife's housekeeping: when the situation is presented in this light it is apparent that no further comment is needed. Figures for 1976 are not yet available but preliminary press reports indicate that it is highly likely that the 1975 picture will be repeated. If so, one must hope that thereafter the general recovery of the economy will permit a return to normality and that in future years we shall be able to look back on 1975 and 1976 as some kind of aberration. In all the comments in newspapers and journals on Britain's economic plight, this particular aspect of deficit financing seems to have received little or no attention.

There must naturally be fears regarding the interest payments which will become due on the increased debt: already the 1975 figures indicate that the trend, which has continued for many years, for the interest payments to decline relative to GNP has been reversed and one must suspect that the interest payments as a percentage of central government current expenditure will rise significantly in the future.

There is one other way in which the statistics for the most recent years represent a significant change. Until 1972, inclusive, the central government each year loaned to local authorities (LAs) and nationalized industries or public corporations (PCs) sums greater than the increase in the central government's borrowing requirement (quite apart from any separate borrowing by LAs and PCs): this means that the central government was only incurring additional debt because of the lending requirements of the LAs and PCs and was not itself directly incurring debt at all. Since 1973, however, this position has changed and the excess of the increase in the national debt over the central government's lending to LAs and PCs has steadily increased, reaching over £5,000 million in 1975.

Both LAs and PCs also borrow in other ways: nationalized industries issue stocks from time to time and these are bought and sold on the Stock Exchange much like any other public sector stock. Local authorities borrow for a variety of capital purposes, primarily for the building of council houses, but also for education, and for the redevelopment of old town centres. The borrowing is done in a variety of ways: in the longest term, stocks are issued in the capital market for long periods of years (not exceeding the expected life of the project to which the loan relates). The Bank of England keeps a queue of local authorities wishing to issue stocks, issues having to be spaced out so that the success of any one issue is fairly assured. A local authority may have to wait some seven or eight years before its turn comes: then its treasurer has a most difficult decision to make (strictly, to advise the lay councillors to make) – failure to go ahead and issue the stock means going back to the bottom of the queue, but the opportunity may have come at a time when interest rates are exceptionally high, or when the local authority has its financial hands full elsewhere. Shorter borrowing is done via debentures, mortgages, bonds and other pieces of paper, including bills: the latter, which for all practical purposes are identical to Treasury Bills, have become extremely important in recent years, as can be seen by their inclusion in the list of securities eligible for the $12\frac{1}{2}$ per cent reserve assets ratio of the commercial banks specified in 'Competition and Credit Control'. For 1976 (1st quarter), local authority bills totalled £407 million, out of £3,529 million borrowing for one year or less, and estimated total debt of some £26,000 million. Much of the shorter borrowing is done via local authority brokers in the City, often affiliated to discount houses, merchant banks, or other institutions. These brokers are most impressive institutions for the effortless way they handle hundreds of telephone calls every working day, each involving the borrowing or lending of thousands (and perhaps millions) of pounds, for overnight, up to seven days, three months, or longer. A harassed local authority treasurer suddenly needing to borrow £100,000 on a Friday afternoon can have the loan arranged on the telephone within ten minutes. In the 1950s and 1960s it was often the case that when a fiscal and monetary package was being used to curb total demand in the economy, it was not applied to local authorities who were able to continue spending and borrowing unhindered. This is less true now and their borrowing is subject to strict controls.[6]

STRUCTURE AND MANAGEMENT

We must now consider the problem of the 'management' of the debt. In this context management refers to the problem of constantly securing sufficient borrowing to cover the total of the current debt, and to the question of arranging such borrowing in ways that will minimize side-effects, notably effects on monetary policy. Throughout the whole of the post-war years the Bank of England has been worried that it might not be able to secure the necessary borrowing. As it once put it: 'The dominant long-term consideration in debt management is to ensure so far as possible that suitable finance is available.[7] In order to put this point in context, we must recall that Britain has a relatively larger debt than any other comparable country and that we have been increasing the debt steadily throughout the years in question; in addition, a large volume of government stock matures each year and it seemed by no means certain that the holders would reinvest the proceeds in other stock. This problem was considered in detail in the Radcliffe Report and one cannot do better than quote from it:

> The most elementary problem of debt management is one that is necessarily solved in some way or other day by day. The previously existing debt, plus any current Exchequer cash deficit, or minus any current Exchequer cash surplus, has to be and is absorbed. Each day the vast majority of holders of Government securities continue to hold those securities at the end of the day, but a fraction of the securities is unloaded, during the day; *this unloaded fraction, and any currently accruing deficit, must be absorbed* either by new holders in the private sector or against release of cash by the monetary authorities. And the same is true of a year's operations: in some way or other the Government's needs are met, and the debt existing at the end of the year must be held by someone, even if this result can only be achieved by allowing cash to constitute a greater part of the debt than before.[8]

The Report later added:

> The debt manager's aim must be to strive for solution by . . . finding an interest rate structure that will ensure the desired structure of the debt. Yet it is not a method that leaves the distribution of resources untouched: as we have seen . . . even if higher interest rates do not promote increased saving (as they perhaps do), they certainly discourage, though slowly and in limited areas, investment in the private sector. A higher rate of interest designed to attract firm holders of Government securities thus operates not only as a protection for the real needs of the public sector but also acts over a period as a force gradually releasing resources from the private sector. It must not be supposed that this implies a conflict between debt policy and employ-

ment policy: it is rather that, in managing the debt, the authorities must resist the temptation to push interest rates so high in order to get the debt firmly held, that they engender a slow but damaging decline in activity.[9]

Some indication of the complications of the task of debt management may be gained from a study of Table 1.6.

Table 1.6 clarifies a number of points relating to the debt: firstly, it indicates that a variety of institutions, companies, and other subscribers, hold an amalgam of long-term and short-dated securities but very little of the debt is held by private individuals (in view of the large sums involved, this is perhaps hardly surprising), and, secondly, only some 11 per cent is placed overseas. This means that the debt of the public sector is owed primarily within the United Kingdom and we need not therefore have any undue fears regarding a drain on our balance of payments caused by external remittances for interest payments. Thirdly, the headings across the columns indicate type of security and here we see that about a fifth of the debt is in Treasury Bills, which are essentially short-term (issued for 91 days), whilst long-term stocks (of over 5 years) comprise some 40 per cent. Non-marketable debt (i.e. National Savings certificates, premium bonds and similar small savings) account for some 15 per cent. Table 1.6 also makes it clear that £13,634 million, some 25 per cent of the total, remains in official hands, mainly within the Bank of England, and therefore does not really constitute debt at all on the effective date: these are monetary pieces of paper of various kinds most of which will be released or issued at some future date. The footnotes to the table indicate how approximate is this whole exercise of assessing the total size of the debt.

Debt management is therefore seen to consist initially of providing a sufficient variety of securities, short-term, long-term, undated, and non-marketable, to appeal to the widest possible range of subscribers, with an appropriate structure of interest rates and prices. In the view of the Bank of England, however, it has also consisted of managing the markets in the various securities to achieve a high degree of stability of interest rates and prices. The official view has been that the banking and financial institutions which purchase large quantities of gilt-edged securities are more interested in market stability for their investments than in any other factor: if the market price rose (and the interest rate fell), went the official reasoning, potential purchasers would be dissuaded. But if the price fell (and the interest rate rose), this too would defer subscribers – for one thing, they might defer investing in the hope of a further price fall. Thus the market was seen as 'perverse'. A further quotation from the Radcliffe Report emphasizes this point:

In the years 1951 to 1957, which we reviewed with the help of the official witnesses as well as others, the authorities abstained from any attempt to

Table 1.6 Estimated Distribution of the National Debt: 31 March 1976 (£m.)
(*[a] percentage of total debt in italics*)

	Total		Treasury bills	Stocks				Non-marketable debt
				Total	Up to 5 years to maturity	Over 5 and up to 15 years	Over 15 years and undated	
Official holdings	13,634	*25·2* [a]	6,021	6,432	2,864	1,590	1,978	1,181
Market holdings								
Public bodies:								
Public corporations	*33*		*–*	*33*	*26*	*5*	*2*	*–*
Local authorities	*21*		*..*	*21*	*4*	*4*	*13*	*..*
Total public bodies	54	*0·1*	*..*	54	30	9	15	*..*
Banking sector:[b]								
Banks	4,084		1,814	2,270	2,026	244		–
National Giro	39		7	32	27	5		–
Discount market	967		898	69	65	4		–
Total banking sector	5,090	*9·5*	2,719	2,371	2,118	253		–

Other financial institutions:							
Insurance companies	6,953		91	6,862	808	1,299	4,755	..
Building societies	2,396		19	2,377	1,930	421	26	—
National Savings Bank, investment account	395		8	387	62	112	213	—
Trustee savings banks, special investment departments	717		—	717	187	357	173	—
Local authority superannuation funds	732		—	732	79	61	592	—
Other public sector superannuation funds	760		9	751	56	331	364	—
Private sector superannuation funds	1,547		7	1,540	251	264	1,025	—
Investment trusts	235		10	225	51	52	122	—
Unit trusts	27		—	27	6	7	14	—
Other	301		202	99	76	3	20	—
Total other financial institutions	14,063	*26·0*	346	13,717	3,506	2,907	7,304	..
Overseas holders:							
International organizations	2,208		47	102	16	86	—	2,059
Central monetary institutions	2,478		1,155	1,323	760	204	359	—
Other	1,647		8	1,629	220	225	1,184	10
Total overseas holders	6,333	*11·7*	1,210	3,054	996	515	1,543	2,069

(Continued overleaf)

(*Table 1.6 Continued*)

	Total		Treasury bills	Stocks				Non-marketable debt
				Total	Up to 5 years to maturity	Over 5 and up to 15 years	Over 15 years and undated	
Other holders:								
Public Trustee and various non-corporate bodies	270		28	239	51	43	145	3
Private funds and trusts	10,192		..	6,186	2,216	1,150	2,820	4,006
Industrial and commercial companies	745		525[c]	216[d]	} 1,972	} 1,555[e]		} 4
Other (residual)	3,660		–	3,311				349
Total other holders	14,867	27.5	553	9,952	4,239	5,713[f]		4,362
						{ 4,910	13,349	
Total market holdings	40,407	74.8	4,828	29,148	10,889			6,431
Total debt	54,041	100.0	10,849	35,580	13,753	6,500	15,327[g]	7,612
of which, nationalized industries' stocks guaranteed by the Government	908			908	684	–	224	

.. not available.
– nil or less than £½ million.
[a] Percentage of total debt in *italics* with some exceptions.
[b] In previous articles the discount market's holdings of stock were shown at nominal values.
[c] The residual after other holders of Treasury bills have been identified; the total may thus include unidentified holdings of other sectors.
[d] Holdings (at book values) of some 200 large companies covered by the Department of Industry's survey of liquid assets.
[e] On the assumption that the banking sector's holdings of long-dated stock are negligible, this figure represents mainly long-dated stock.
[f] On the assumption made in [e] above, this figure comprises about £1,230 million medium-dated and £4,490 million long-dated.
[g] Of which undated £3,381 million.
Source: 'Distribution of the national debt at end-March 1976', *Bank of England Quarterly Bulletin*, December 1976, p. 449.

stimulate the demand for long bonds by dropping their prices (i.e. raising interest rates) because they believed not merely that there would be no expansion of demand, but that demand would actually shrink if the authorities so openly and deliberately tried to push their sales. They based their policy primarily on the view that a deliberate drop in prices would create expectations of a further drop, but also on a more general fear that rising interest rates were 'damaging to Government credit', and therefore restrictive of future possibilities of sales of Government securities. In thinking in terms of 'Government credit' the authorities were, as was repeatedly emphasized to us, thinking of overseas confidence in sterling as well as the future demand for Government securities.[10]

The Report went on to express doubts about whether there was a direct link between creditworthiness and interest rates and then continued:

A more substantial fear is that a drop in bond prices, especially if it appears to be the result of deliberate action, may be repeated; to the extent that this happens, a rise in interest rates will not increase but will reduce the demand for bonds. 'It can be argued', as the Governor of the Bank said, 'that there is always a price at which buyers will appear. That is doubtless true, but the price might be a long way down, much damage might be done on the way . . .' The evidence we have heard from financial institutions supports the Governor's judgment, and we accept it. It has, however, to be remembered that he was judging markets as they have been functioning in this decade, that their behaviour has been conditioned by the circumstances of the time, and that one of these circumstances has been a lack of contact between the minds of the authorities and the minds of outside operators and commentators. If the intentions of the authorities could be more generally understood – and this would involve the fostering of greater understanding outside official circles – there would be less danger of exaggerated or perverse reactions in the market when the authorities took a step designed to tighten their hold on liquidity.[11]

Not until *Competition and Credit Control*, October 1971, did the Bank of England abandon its policy of daily intervention in the markets, and then its resolve lasted just nine months: with the June 1972 sterling crisis the financial markets were in turmoil (the interest rate in the inter-bank market, for example, reached 160 per cent) and the Bank once again intervened to restore stability.

IMPACT ON MONETARY POLICY

The second major aspect of debt management relates to the effects on the government's monetary policy, primarily via the advances of the commercial banks. Monetary policy in the post-war years has been based on the view that bank credit, which of its very nature must be expansionary, has depended on the banks' liquidity in general and on their holdings of

Treasury Bills in particular: the greater their holdings of Treasury Bills and other short-dated stocks, the greater would be their ability to lend to their customers.[12] (Such a formulation also fits in with the monetarist view of economic policy: since the Money Supply is defined to include cash plus sums in bank accounts, including bank loans and overdrafts, an undue expansion of the Money Supply might follow from a budget deficit.) Therefore if the Bank of England was to avoid undue credit creation with its inherent inflationary consequences, it had to endeavour constantly to restructure the debt towards stocks and away from bills. Further, since any debt gradually shortens in length as time passes, a degree of 'funding' was always required if liquidity was not to increase: funding refers to the process of replacing maturing bills or bonds by longer-dated stock. At the same time the authorities have naturally wished to keep the interest payments on the debt as low as possible in order to minimize the current burden of servicing the debt.

It is therefore apparent that throughout the last thirty years the operation of monetary policy has been severely circumscribed by the necessities of debt management. The use of open market operations, in particular, effectively was not possible for long periods when a substantial residue of borrowing had to be done via Treasury Bills which were largely taken up by the discount market, thus affecting the banks' liquidity positions. This partly explains the recourse to alternative instruments of control such as the directives to banks and special deposits and it was no coincidence that *Competition and Credit Control* in 1971, with its emphasis on the increased use of open market operations and the abolition of directives to banks, came just after the two years of reductions in debt referred to above. As already indicated, the new control system broke down in the sterling crisis of 1972 and a new directive to the banks (now called a 'letter of guidance') was issued in August, 1972.

The steady increase in the debt in the post-war years must also have had a generally upward effect on interest rates but it seems probable that the rising trend in interest rates should be related more to the inflationary situation and to world liquidity shortages than to the needs of the debt.

Mention should be made here of the 'New Cambridge' view that, over a period of years, public sector deficits must logically be directly linked to deficits on the balance of payments, but as yet this view has had little effect on official policy.[13]

'BURDEN' ARGUMENTS

The final topic we need to consider relates to the theoretical and sometimes philosophical arguments as to whether the debt constitutes an intolerable burden. In the 1950s there arose a school of thought, led by

Professor J. M. Buchanan, which argued that it was quite unjustifiable for the present generation constantly to incur additional debt to bequeath to future generations. Their central argument was that if we bequeath to our children additional capital assets, unmatched by any extra debt, we shall clearly earn their gratitude in future years but if we leave behind us both extra assets and extra debt we lay ourselves open to severe criticism from the generations as yet unborn. These arguments were discussed by such writers as E. J. Mishan, W. G. Bowen, R. G. Davis, D. H. Kopf and F. Modigliani and the ensuing debate became both complex and acrimonious: only a brief summary is possible here.

Clearly future generations would be in a *relatively* preferable position if they inherited the same volume of assets and no extra debt but this would be unlikely to happen: without the recourse to deficit financing the level of public sector investment would almost certainly fall considerably. This would mean a slower growth of GNP and living standards and a smaller inheritance for future generations. Therefore in *absolute* terms they would be worse off. The debate therefore hinged on whether the 'burden' of having to meet the interest payments on the debt (and presumably paying off the capital value of the debt one day) were fully compensated by the relevant capital assets. In Modigliani's view the answer depends on whether we are using scarce economic resources in the most efficient way possible – but presumably this is always a valid point in economics and has little directly to do with the debt.

A further point is that if one section of the debt is amortized at some particular date in the future, an undue penalty might be imposed on the taxpayers at that time. It is also possible to envisage present consumers being deprived by the fact that scarce resources (e.g. labour) are being devoted to the production of capital goods (e.g. a power station) the benefits from which will only become available at some date in the future. This point, however, presumably applies to a greater or less extent to all investment expenditure and does not relate directly to the debt. Finally we may envisage a particular burden on the national economy in so far as we borrow from overseas since the external remittance of interest payments will constitute a drain on the balance of payments in future years. Here the reply is that by borrowing overseas we obtain the use of scarce financial capital which might otherwise have to be diverted from private sector investment at home. In any event, as seen above, the greater part of the debt is not in fact borrowed externally.

The theoretical arguments as to whether the debt constitutes a 'burden', in whatever sense, are much more complex than can be indicated in a short summary and the interested reader is urged to pursue them elsewhere.[14]

REFERENCES

1. *The Times*, 16 December 1976.
2. *Bank of England Quarterly Bulletin*, 'Distribution of the national debt at end-March 1974', Vol 14, No. 4, December 1974, p. 433.
3. *Report of the Committee on the Working of the Monetary System*, Cmnd. 827, 1959, para. 69, p. 22.
4. *See*, for example, J. C. R. Dow, *The Management of the British Economy*, Cambridge University Press, 1974.
5. *See* J. R. Hough, 'French Economic Policy', *National Westminster Bank Review*, May 1976.
6. *See* N. Hepworth, *The Finance of Local Government*, Allen & Unwin, 1971.
7. Cited in C. D. Cohen, *British Economic Policy 1960–69*, Butterworths, 1971, p. 100.
8. Report, *op. cit.*, para. 558, pp. 206–7.
9. *ibid.*, para. 561, pp. 207–8.
10. *ibid.*, para. 564, pp. 208–9.
11. *ibid.*, para. 565, p. 209.
12. *See* H. G. Johnson (ed.), *Readings in British Monetary Economics*, O.U.P., 1972.
13. *See* D. Kern, 'Monetary aspects of the current economic debate', *National Westminster Bank Review*, August 1975, pp. 6–17.
14. *See* the six relevant articles in R. W. Houghton (ed.), *Public Finance* Penguin, 1970, and Chapter 5 in E. J. Mishan, *21 Popular Economic Fallacies*, Pelican, 1969.

QUESTIONS FOR DISCUSSION

1. The case study makes clear that more adequate statistics are required. But this would mean engaging more civil servants. Would this be desirable in the present state of the economy?
2. Discuss the change in attitudes to economic policy advocated by Keynes and its implications for the debt.
3. How worrying is the changed picture for 1974 and subsequently? Is deficit financing to meet *current* spending a major problem? If so, why?
4. Discuss whether the Bank of England's fears about the 'perverseness' of the market for government stock were exaggerated.
5. Have the problems of debt management seriously interfered with monetary policy and curtailed the Bank of England's freedom of action?

6. What is the link between deficit financing and an increase in the Money Supply?

7. Discuss the advantages and disadvantages of leaving LAs and PCs relatively free to incur deficits if they wish, or of subjecting them to strict controls by the central government.

8. What general effects on the national economy might follow from an increase in interest rates? In what circumstances would the government find such an increase (i) desirable and (ii) undesirable. What would be the effect on the servicing costs of the debt?

9. Why do significant quantities of various government stocks remain within the public sector at any one time?

10. Why did the budget surpluses in 1969 and 1970 make it easier for the new banking control system, *Competition and Credit Control,* to come into force in October 1971?

11. How convincing do you find the arguments that the debt constitutes a 'burden':
    (i) on future generations, and
    (ii) on our balance of payments?

The Economics of Scottish Independence

BACKGROUND

The Scottish National Party was founded in 1934, from an amalgamation of smaller groups and has, as its prime objective, the securing of 'an independent Scotland within the Commonwealth with the Queen as Head of State'. It would be fair to say that the growth of the debate on Scottish independence has tended to follow the growth of electoral support for the SNP, which since the 1960s has been one of steady increase in votes at each successive general election. Of immediate relevance is the answer to the question: is Scotland economically viable as an independent country?

The basic arguments supporting the negative answer to this question can be summarized in the propositions that Scotland is too poor (McCrone 1969), too dominated (Firn, 1975) and, in contrast to the first proposition, too rich (Smallwood, 1976). In this case study each argument for and against the economic viability of Scottish independence will be examined. This, it must be stressed, is an exercise in economic analysis and not a case study on the desirability or otherwise of independence.

SCOTLAND TOO POOR 1

It may be as well to quote an extract from Gavin McCrone's book to put the overall debate into perspective.

> Many people start discussion of the economics of nationalism by asking if Scotland could be self supporting. This is an absurd question . . . Scotland has a highly industrialized economy with a gross domestic product per head which, though slightly less than England's nevertheless makes her comparable with other European countries. She is therefore among the more advanced nations of the world economically. She is clearly much wealthier than the Republic of Ireland and a thousand times more able to look after herself than Basutoland, which nonetheless manages to be independent. If Scotland becomes independent, no doubt a variety of adjustments would have to be made; some of which might be drastic and painful; but if Scotland wanted to be independent, there is obviously no question of her being unable to afford it economically. (McCrone, 1969, p. 52.)

Scotland in McCrone's view was better off remaining inside the United Kingdom and thereby benefiting from the support of a richer partner.

He went on to assert that Scotland received more in government expenditure than it contributed in taxation revenue, using information for 1967. The budgetary deficit he found to be £211 millions out of an expenditure total of £1,343 million, i.e. about 16 per cent. Total government revenue collected in Scotland in 1967 was £1,095 million and expenditure was £1,343 million.

McCrone wrote:

. . . if Scotland were to take over responsibility for the bill which public expenditure presents in (the) accounts, she would either have to raise taxes sharply or engage in substantial Government borrowing. (McCrone, 1969, p. 62.)

McCrone made the valid point that it was natural, in a Union, for the richer parts of the community to assist the poorer parts. Scotland's gross domestic product per head in 1967 was 93 per cent of that of England's, and over the years a similar percentage difference had been experienced between the two countries.

Independence would force a Scottish government to raise taxes or borrowing to cover the deficit or to reduce public expenditure by that amount. Neither alternative was politically palatable; both alternatives reduced living standards which were already below those of England.

The arguments against McCrone's conclusions can be summarized briefly. The first, and probably major one, was that Scotland's economy while tied to, or controlled by, the United Kingdom government had to accept whatever stabilization measures it was found necessary to impose because of the UK balance of payments and foreign exchange problems. Post-war economic management had resorted to 'Stop-Go' economic policies to reduce activity in periods of balance of payments deficit (with its consequent pressure on the international parity of the sterling exchange rate) and to increase activity when unemployment had cooled the economy down and brought the balance of payments into surplus, or close to it. The stop-go cycle badly affected the generally lower level of activity in Scotland (unemployment rates tended to be about double England's throughout the whole cycle) because the 'stop' phase deepened the permanent Scottish recession and the 'go' phase was never strong enough to relieve it. Thus, Scotland's per capita output was always below its potential. If Scotland had pursued independent economic policies it would have run its economy at a higher level of activity than permitted in the UK system and this would have produced a greater taxable capacity to sustain public expenditure at the levels of the 1960s.

In so far as rising money incomes produce rising tax contributions (buoyancy) at the same rate of tax it is a feasible argument in theory but whether incomes would rise high enough, even taking up all the unemployed Scots, to reduce the deficit substantially is another matter. However, a reduction in unemployment would reduce public expenditure on unemployment, and associated social security payments. A deficit would remain if it was not found possible to raise economic activity because of structural deficiencies in the Scottish economy. This latter was a subject of considerable debate in the 1960s among regional economists (Johnston, *et al.*, 1971).

Another line of attack on McCrone concentrated on the Unallocated Expenditure items in his accounts. Certain central government expenditures cannot be attributed to regions because they are by their nature *public* goods; once provided everybody benefits from them irrespective of whether they contribute towards their costs or not. Defence, and the provision of British Embassies throughout the world, are examples of public goods. The costs of such provision can only be allocated on a population basis and this is what McCrone did in his book. The total of these items came to £291 million. Because their attribution is arbitrary it left open the question of whether a Scottish government would spend this amount on its own defence and external relations.

In short a Scottish government may spend its budget in a different way to that of a UK government, increasing some items and reducing others. In so far as, for example, defence expenditure was reduced and what was spent was spent *in* Scotland this would have different economic effects to attributed defence expenditure at 1967 levels, much of it spent in England and Germany (Kennedy, 1976a).

The budgetary deficit of £211 million for 1967 did not present a decisive case against Scottish independence but it did raise important questions of how to cope with the deficit. Available statistical information did not go very far in providing definite answers.

SCOTLAND TOO POOR 2

The non-availability of statistics for important aspects of the Scottish economy has already been mentioned. This is not surprising. It is not usual for the economy to collect statistics for each of its constituent economic regions as if they were separate countries. Thus, the trade flows between each region and between the regions and the rest of the world are not collected by the UK government. Yet this information would be of immense interest in the debate on the economic viability of Scottish independence. Scotland trades with other parts of the United Kingdom and with the rest of the world. Without information on this trade a large gap is left in the total picture of the workings of the Scottish economy.

The Fraser of Allander Institute for Research on the Scottish Economy, at the University of Strathclyde, is working on the construction of a trade flow series for Scotland using Input–Output techniques. Until this is available it is necessary to use indirect techniques which in the nature of things are unreliable and must be treated with extreme caution.

One such method is to manipulate social accounting identities. The basic principle behind social accounting is quite simple. The sum of all *incomes* received in a community is its *national income*. This must equal (allowing for errors in computation and imputation) the sum of the *value added* in each stage of production, which is the *national output*. This, in turn, must equal (subject to the same caveat) the sum of all *outlays* in the community, which is the *national expenditure*.

The standard social accounting identity is in the form:

$$Y = C + I + G + (X - M) - (T - S)$$

where Y = income, C = consumption, I = investment, G = government, X = exports, M = imports, T = indirect taxes and S = subsidies (Beckerman, 1968; Yanovsky, 1965).

The domestic output of a country is its *domestic product* and the output of residents is its *national product*; the difference between these is known as the *net property income from abroad*. In some countries, and in constituent parts of the same country – taking other constituent parts as composed of non-residents – net property income can be significant.

Just as the trade flows between constituent parts of an economy are not normally recorded it is as difficult to discover the net property incomes of a constituent economic region. In the case of Scotland there are no figures available for either trade flows or net property income from abroad (especially as England in this context must be counted as being 'abroad'). Hence, it is not possible to calculate Scotland's Gross *National* Product. It is possible to calculate its Gross *Domestic* Product. From the Gross Domestic Product it is possible to estimate, crudely, the trade balance by calculating everything else in the social accounting identity and treating the residual as the value of $(X - M)$. But as the real balance of trade includes net property income from abroad – which might in fact eliminate any deficit on trade, as it did in the case of the United Kingdom up to 1972 – it cannot be but an incomplete picture of the balance of trade between Scotland and the rest of the world.

The technique of using the residual in the identity is unreliable for another reason. The actual estimates of the other elements in the identity $(Y, C, I, G, T, S,)$ may be in error. The methods of computation are not strictly accurate and the errors may be substantial, in either direction. However, all caveats considered, the method does give us the only 'trade series' available, which can with suitable care be used as a guide to the real situation.

A trade balance, using the above technique, has been calculated (Begg, Lythe, Sorley, 1975) for Scotland 1961–71. It is presented in T1.bae 2.1

Table 2.1 Scotland's 'Balance of Trade' 1961-71

	Current Prices	
	Total (£m.)	Per Head (£)
1961	−200	−39
1962	−151	−29
1963	−177	−34
1964	−239	−46
1965	−216	−41
1966	−220	−42
1967	−259	−50
1968	−381	−73
1969	−401	−77
1970	−405	−78
1971	−444	−85

Source: H. M. Begg, C. M. Lythe, R. Sorley, *Expenditure in Scotland* 1961–1971, Scottish Academic Press, 1975, p. 166, Table 5.111.

Using estimates for Scotland's Gross Domestic Product for each year Begg, Lythe and Sorley calculated the difference with their estimates for Scottish Gross Domestic Expenditure. For each year in question there was a deficit. Whatever the actual figures, on the crude trade measure, Scotland was in deficit with the rest of the world, even in periods when the United Kingdom was in substantial surplus with the rest of the world. Because of Scotland's small population in relation to its deficit (5 million people) the per capita deficit was substantially greater than the per capita trade deficit for the United Kingdom (55 million) during this period.

There is also the direction of trade flows to be considered. Scotland's trade with the rest of the world, excluding England and Wales, is subject to different economic forces from its trade with the rest of the United Kingdom. Scottish whisky is one of Britain's largest dollar earners and it makes a substantial contribution to the UK balance of payments. Likewise, England itself is a large market for whisky which in the event of independence would become an export earner for Scotland. Trade within a customs union, such as the United Kingdom, developed over many years is bound to be trade diverting as well as trade creating. If, as a result of UK economic policies, Scotland is compelled to follow policies that work against trade creation with the rest of the world and in favour of trade diversion to the rest of the UK it may be that its balance of trade is affected in an unfavourable way. This is one of the considerations put forward in discussing the merits of customs unions, such as the EEC, and it has every bit as much relevance for a discussion on the merits of Scotland remaining in a customs union with England.

Alternative economic policies to those at present pursued within the United Kingdom might include measures to increase agricultural output, extend fishing limits, re-equip some basic industrial sectors, adjust energy policies (particularly in electricity production of which Scotland already has surplus capacity), and invest in newer technologies.

SCOTLAND TOO DOMINATED

As an economic region of the United Kingdom, Scotland has received special attention in the form of regional economic policies designed to stimulate the local economy and to counteract the decline in certain manufacturing sectors. All governments since the war have pursued regional policies of one kind or another. One instrument in these policies has been the use of Industrial Development Certificates to limit industrial and manufacturing expansion in the relatively well-off parts of England, and another has been the use of investment incentives and grants to persuade companies to locate in the development areas, of which Scotland is one of the largest. The result over the years has been the location of many companies and their operations in Scotland which would otherwise, in the main, have sited their plants elsewhere in the UK, or, perhaps, Europe.

A direct consequence of this kind of regional policy has been the growth of external managerial control of decisive sectors of the Scottish economy. The head office of a company, or holding company of subsidiaries, is the place where decisions about expansion, contraction, investment, employment, pricing, technology and the share-out of contracts are made. If that head office is sited outside a particular country, or region, it follows that these decisions are not necessarily made with the specific or broader interests of the place where the branch plants are sited as a major consideration. Of equal importance, and in some cases, of even greater importance, the decision centres of these companies may not be open to pressure or persuasion from the government of the country where their branch factories operate and could actually pursue policies in respect of their operations that run counter to the declared policies or objectives of the government concerned.

Research conducted at Glasgow University (Firn, 1976) has provided quantitative data on the extent to which the Scottish economy is dominated by external managerial control. These detail the extent of external control in manufacturing sectors of the Scottish economy for 1973. The survey covered 3,000 manufacturing enterprises in Scotland which between them account for the majority of plants and all the major ones

Indigenous Scottish control of manufacturing sectors runs from a mere 7·8 per cent of the electrical engineering industry to 88 per cent of the relatively unimportant leather, leather goods and fur sector, which only covers 0·5 per cent of Scottish manufacturing employment. In contrast

English-controlled plants in Scotland account for the 12 per cent balance of the leather industry and up to 80 per cent of the coal and petroleum sector. In the case of the Scottish instrument engineering sector 60 per cent is in the hands of companies whose head offices are across the Atlantic. In all, English companies control five sectors outright (petroleum, chemicals, metal manufacturing, electrical engineering, motor vehicles) and have substantial (over a third) shares in five others.

The findings brought out some crucial aspects of the dominance by external companies. These are:

Only 41 per cent of manufacturing employment in Scotland is controlled internally.
The larger the enterprise, the more likely it is to be controlled externally.
Over one quarter of total manufacturing employment is in non-local branch plants.
110 enterprises account for 46 per cent of total manufacturing employment.
The faster growing the sector the lower is the amount of Scottish participation.
The five fastest growing sectors have less than 14 per cent of indigenous control. (Firn, 1975, pp. 162–3.)

Firn's conclusions are somewhat pessimistic for an independent Scottish economic policy (though he does not exclude its desirability).

The economic relationship between branch factories and subsidiaries and their head offices or sister plants in other countries is not a straightforward one. Many of these plants purchase most of their requirements from outside Scotland. (Lever, 1974 – quoted in Firn 1975, p. 164), and many sell most of their output outside Scotland. In addition inter-branch sales and purchases can involve transfer pricing. This is a device by which multinational companies manipulate internal pricing between their subsidiaries to arrange things so that the bulk of their profits appears in their companies which are located in countries where the profit taxation levels are most favourable. For this reason a multinational company may run a Scottish operation at a book-loss so as to avoid profit tax in the United Kingdom. Naturally, there is more than a loss of taxation revenue involved; by understating the value of exports and overstating the value of imports (including licences for company-owned patents) the trade flows of a country could appear to be worse than they are in fact. This practice is an element of the problem which a country, with a large proportion of its economic activity controlled externally, has to face when it attempts to pursue an independent economic policy. Firn suggests that the problem in Scotland's case is so serious that it would make it 'almost impossible for an independent Scottish government to run an independent economic policy' and that 'the power of Scotland to shape or strongly influence her own economic future, has been, is being, and probably will continue to be, strongly eroded' (Firn, 1975, pp. 164–5).

The problem of external control is not confined to Scotland alone. It is being experienced in the United Kingdom as a whole and in many European and Third World countries. The decisive question is whether in Scotland's case the trend has gone on so long that it is now virtually irreversible.

One possible solution, which will be discussed in the next section in its proper context, is the use of oil revenues, surplus to the immediate absorptive capacity of the Scottish economy, to buy out external control of selected manufacturing enterprises. In concert with this policy it is possible to conceive of legislation that requires companies to have majority Scottish participation in their ownership and management (this has been introduced in Canada, Australia, Japan, Mexico among other places) and which imposes accountancy practices that forbid transfer pricing.

SCOTLAND TOO RICH

1972 was the big, though at the time unheralded, turning point in the economic debate on independence. From that year on the prospect, or spectre, of oil dominates the discussion. The vast oil finds, off the coast of Scotland, are worth, according to official estimates, over £200 billion at 1975 prices. Anticipated government taxation revenues from the oil flow are expected to be worth about £3 billion a year by 1980. (Table 2.2) (Kemp, 1976; MacKay, 1975 and 1976; McRae, 1976). These kinds of sums clearly more than cover a Scottish government's revenue deficit on government account of £211 million a year and a trade deficit of £400 million a year on the balance of payments.

Table 2.2 Oil Company Profits, Government Royalties and Taxation, 1975–80 from Scottish North Sea Oil

	1975	1976	1977	1978	1979	1980
Total Sales Revenue* of which	209	986	2095	3186	4818	5534
Company Revenues**	183	863	1186	1739	2355	2191
Royalties	26	123	262	398	602	692
Tax	0	0	647	1049	1861	2651
Total Government Take	26	123	909	1447	2463	3343

Source: D. I. MacKay and G. A. Mackay, *The Political Economy of North Sea Oil*, Martin Robertson, London, 1975, Table 5.4, p. 99.

* Valued at $11 (US) per barrel.

** After royalties and corporation tax but before operating costs.

What happens if the world oil price falls? While Scottish oil costs are greatly in excess of the per barrel costs of oil in the Middle East the world oil price would have to tumble a long way down (to under $5 per barrel) before the viability of these fields was in doubt (MacKay, 1975).

Another question, sometimes raised, is more concerned with politics and international law than with economics but it is as well to dispose of it at this point. Would an independent Scotland own the North Sea oilfields? International law would suggest that the answer would be yes.

The United Kingdom's jurisdiction in the North Sea is recognized in international law. British law establishes these rights in the Continental Shelf Act of 1964 and it is under this act that current exploration and exploitation is operated. In 1968 the UK government passed a Continental Shelf (Jurisdictional) Order which divided the UK zone of the North Sea along the parallel of latitude 55° 50'. The north sector was designated as the Scottish area of jurisdiction, under which Scottish Law would apply (*see* Royal Scottish Geographical Society, 1973).

Suggestions have been made that the boundary line would have to be changed to reflect the actual boundary between Scotland and England. The boundary would then run in a roughly north-easterly direction instead of along a parallel of latitude. However, it would not run far enough north-easterly to take in the most southerly of the oilfields yet discovered. If it was run even more to the north it would take in only a few of the smallest fields; to take in the large fields (Forties, for instance) it would need to be almost vertical, thus, breaking with any alignment with the land boundary, and in these circumstances subject to consultation and negotiation between the two governments (MacKay, 1975).

The sheer size of the oil revenues in relation to Scotland is quite staggering. The Gross Domestic Product of Scotland in 1973 was approximately £5·35 billion, or 8·6 per cent of the UK's G.D.P. of £62·2 billion. The oil revenues, net of oil imports, operating expenditures and remitted profits, could be in the order of 2 per cent of the 1973 Scottish G.D.P. in 1976, 31 per cent in 1978 and 68 per cent in 1980.

The independence debate has now shifted to entirely new ground. No longer is it a question of Scotland having to adjust its living standards downwards (itself a controversial proposition) but one of having to suffer economic difficulties because of the very size of the oil revenues in relation to the capacity of the Scottish economy. Scotland is, in effect, too rich to be economically independent (Smallwood, 1975; Labour Party, 1976)!

In Table 2.3 there is an oil balance of payments for Scotland for 1974–80. From 1976 the oil balance swings into the black and climbs from then on towards £3,651 million in 1980. What the actual balance of payments will look like through those years will depend on the real balance of trade, including net property income from abroad, and the domestic policies that are followed by the government. It is on speculating about what such a government would do, or be compelled to do, that the opponents of independence have concentrated their criticism (Smallwood, 1975). They have elaborated upon a scenario that shows that Scotland

Table 2.3 'Oil' Balance of Payments of an Independent Scotland 1974–80 (£m)

		1974	1975	1976	1977	1978	1979	1980
1	Exports (oil)		209	986	2095	3186	4818	5534
2	Imports (oil)	336	339	342	339	339	355	368
3	Imports equipment and services	563	759	876	810	728	630	543
4	Import content operating costs		6	27	57	87	131	151
5	Visible trade balance (1)−[(2)+(3)+(4)]	−899	−895	−259	+889	+2032	+3702	+4472
6	Invisibles: profits remitted	0	148	696	896	1304	1725	1519
7	Current Balance (1)−[(2)+(3)+(4) +(6)]	−899	−1043	−955	−7	+728	+1977	+2953
8	Inward Investment	675	923	1080	1013	923	810	698
9	Balance of current and capital accounts (1)+(8)−[(2)+(3) +(4)+(6)]	−224	−120	+125	+1006	+1651	+2787	+3651

Source: D. I. MacKay and G. A. Mackay, *The Political Economy of North Sea Oil*, Martin Robertson, London, 1975, Table 8.1, p. 172

Note: Assumptions made include:
    (a) oil valued at $11 a barrel.
    (b) Scotland's oil consumption 10% of UK's.
    (c) 25–30% of North Sea oil goods and services produced in Scotland.
    (d) 70% of operating expenditures accrues directly to companies operating in Scotland.
    (e) 10% of capital and operating expenditures financed from Scottish sources.
    (f) 90% of profits remitted outside Scotland.

would have a slightly higher standard of living as a result of the oil, at least initially, with a higher level of unemployment and an acceleration in the decline of its manufacturing sector.

THE SMALLWOOD SCENARIO

Scotland's economic problems can be summarized as a persistent and relatively high level of unemployment, a steady loss of jobs in agriculture, mining, manufacturing, transport and distribution, an inadequate growth in alternative employment opportunities, a high level of migration and the largest concentration of areas of multiple deprivation in the UK (Table 2.4) (Johnston, 1971). Scottish incomes were, until recently, about 8 per cent less than the UK average. The oil construction boom (creating about 50,000 higher-wage jobs) and the UK recession have narrowed the differential – and in some quarters actually reversed it – but as the construction boom fades and the UK moves from recession to recovery the earlier pattern should reassert itself.

Table 2.4 Approximate Employment Losses and Gains in Scotland 1964–74, Selected Main Sectors

Sector	Losses	Gains
Agriculture, forestry and fishing	34,500	
Mining and quarrying	31,000	
Manufacturing	35,000	
Transport, communications	27,000	
Distributive trades	29,000	
Other	10,000	
Professional, scientific services		87,000
Public administration		27,000
Insurance, banking, finance		20,000
Manufacturing		19,000
Other		8,000
Totals	166,500	161,000

Source: Department of Employment (Scottish Office, 1976).

Given that a persistent labour surplus 'is commonly a sign that a country's industries are prevented by foreign competition from expanding fast enough to absorb the available labour' (McCrone, 1969) it follows that Scotland's industries are in decline (job losses exceed job gains) because of the relatively lower productivity per worker compared to, say, England, and other European competitors. It is worth noting that a similar table was presented by McCrone (1969) to argue that Scotland would not be better off with independence because of its poor competitiveness, its need but inability (due to retaliatory action by England) to devalue the Scots pound and the deficits on revenue and trade accounts. The same table is now presented to support the same conclusion that Scotland would be worse off in conditions of substantial resource availability to raise productivity, substantial surplus of revenue and trade accounts and the tendency for a Scots pound to revalue.

Independence without the oil means that Scotland is lumbered with a structural imbalance in its employment pattern – too heavy a dependence on declining industries – and independence with the oil means that Scotland is burdened by a rising exchange value of its currency against competitors which invites a flood of imports and would accelerate the decline of the already declining industries. That both scenarios lead to the proposition that Scotland would be better off remaining inside the United Kingdom, with the oil revenues accruing to a British government, and the continuation of regional assistance policies to mitigate the structural problems of Scotland, is interesting but not convincing. The debate can only be settled in a comparison between the relative problems for Scotland from remaining inside the British economy and the problems arising from withdrawing.

Both McCrone and Smallwood are in favour of devolution within the

United Kingdom. Both see devolution as leading to an improvement in Scotland's relative position and not just to a continuation of the past. This must mean that the British Government would increase the flow of resources to Scotland to regenerate the economy, change the structural imbalance and permit, through a Scottish Assembly, the necessary political direction to give institutional push to these changes. In other words, Scotland within the UK would be able to gain real benefits from the increased economic strength of Britain, resulting in part from the North Sea oil revenues, without having to suffer from the side-effects of the oil flow into a small economy.

The basic question remains, however: can the same result be achieved by independence? This boils down to a question of whether Scotland can absorb enough of the oil revenues to finance full employment and whether it is able to cope with the surplus oil revenues. Devolution and independence are alternative solutions to this question; the former involves increasing regional assistance and creaming off the surplus oil revenues for British central government purposes and the latter involves increasing domestic economic activity to the full employment level and recycling the surplus according to the arrangements negotiated by a sovereign parliament in Edinburgh. By definition both alternatives are economically viable; the question as to which will be chosen is a political one.

Past experience of British regional economic policy as applied to Scotland has been that it has never reached a sufficient scale to bring about full employment – Scottish rates have remained at about twice the UK rate since the 1930s – and this must imply a considerable increase in the resource transfer to Scotland from the rest of the UK if devolution is to work (Begg, 1976; Lee, 1973). In the context of an oil revenue flow of £3 billion a year to the UK government this must mean that some proportion of the oil revenues will be used to finance this resource transfer. The extent, and the character, of that use of the oil revenues will remain a responsibility of the UK government under devolution. If the UK decides that there are other pressing claims on the oil revenues (international debts, regional deprivation in other parts of the UK, public sector borrowing requirements, deficits on the balance of payments or whatever) the Scottish economy will have to wait its turn, as in the past.

What could a Scottish government do to deal with the structural and demand-deficient level of economic activity and how could it avoid the problems of revenue abundance raised by Smallwood?

We can begin by outlining what it ought *not* to do. If it used the oil revenues to raise domestic consumption, perhaps in response to trade union pressure and high consumer expectations of the immediate fruits of an oil-financed independence, it would be able to increase effective demand towards the level of full employment output. Assuming no other problems, such as on the exchange rate, this would transform the oil as a capital asset into personal consumption. In effect Scotland would consume its capital asset with no long-term change in its economy, except to make the structural imbalance even worse by de-industrializing its manufacturing sector.

If the exchange rate of the Scottish pound rose against the English pound, and other currencies, the above situation would be reached more rapidly. A rising exchange value has two main effects. It raises the foreign price of domestic exports and reduces the domestic price of imports. The former will exacerbate the competitive disadvantage of Scottish exports, thus reducing them in volume, and the latter will increase the substitution of domestic manufacturing activity by imports. Scotland's export industries will decline (creating unemployment in them) and Scotland's domestic manufacturing sector will also decline (creating more unemployment). Scotland, in effect will de-industrialize more quickly even if it can finance its standard of living with oil revenues for the duration of the oil flow (Smallwood, 1975; Labour Party, 1976).

THE SIMPSON PLAN

If Scotland was to do what the above scenario requires of it then independence 'would not be worth the candle' (Smallwood, 1975) but then this would represent such a monumental mistake in economic policy that the economic managers would have to be either grossly incompetent or wilfully malevolent. An alternative strategy has been outlined which avoids the pitfalls of Smallwood's scenario and increases economic activity (Simpson, 1976).

The major aim of the Simpson Plan is to transform the capital asset of oil into another capital asset (physical investment in manufacturing industry). The use of oil revenues for consumption will need to be strictly limited. This does not preclude a rise in living standards it only alters the source of the increase. This transformation can be accomplished in a way that meets England's requirements for the foreign exchange earned by oil exports and the increased economic activity in its manufacturing sector.

Scotland and England would open a joint bank account into which the proceeds of oil exports (net of Scottish taxation) would be placed. Scotland became self-sufficient in oil in June 1976 and hence all additional levels of oil output are exportable. (Indeed, North Sea oil is chemically more suited to Continental requirements than those of the UK.) The Bank of England would be able to draw foreign exchange from the joint account to meet its international obligations or whatever else it requires foreign currency for. On withdrawing such funds it would immediately deposit in the joint account an equivalent amount of pound sterling at an exchange rate agreed between the two countries. The Central Bank of Scotland would be free to draw on these sterling deposits to finance its economic strategy. It would agree not to convert these sterling balances into foreign currency but would undertake to use them in expenditures within England and the sterling area.

The sterling deposits held by Scotland in the joint account would be used to:

1. to purchase physical goods and technical services from England to re-equip and modernize the Scottish manufacturing sector;
2. to purchase existing assets in Scotland owned by companies operating from England by outright take-over or majority stake;
3. to loan back to the English government at an agreed rate of interest.

The results of these activities would be to counter the structural imbalance and relative lower productivity of Scottish industry. The expansion of net investment would be a factor in Scotland's economic growth. As long as the imports of physical capital goods can be matched to the current pool of unemployed labour, and the labour 'shaken out' by rising productivity in other plants and sectors, Scotland can achieve full employment and economic growth. The gradual acquisition of control over manufacturing industry would reduce the problem of external control of the Scottish economy (Firn, 1975). If this was accompanied by the acquisition of higher technology, fully integrated research and development functions alongside manufacturing and the development of growth sectors it would alter the structural balance and lead to a more competitive economy.

England would gain from access to a supply of foreign currency (which is England's main interest in North Sea Oil) and benefit from an expansion of manufactured exports to Scotland. The resource transfer would be assured rather than dependent on the political will of a UK government. In effect, what is happening in this plan, is the resource transfer is taking place in such a way that Scotland overcomes its basic economic problems of unemployment, low productivity and declining manufacturing sectors (the present objective of regional policies) and England is receiving the twin benefits of the foreign exchange earnings of oil and an export-led boom. If the resource transfer results in too high a level of activity in England the English government can take sterling out of the joint account by means of sterling loans.

The remaining problem concerns the Scottish exchange rate. The tendency for this to rise can be countered by established methods of exchange control. The availability of the oil revenues in the joint account would assist England in maintaining its exchange rate against other countries. As the net investment programme gets under way in Scotland it will increase man-hour productivity and reduce unit costs of export output. This will counter the price changes resulting from any modest increase in the exchange rate. If such increases do take place the net effect of them must be considered: as imports fall in price this must reduce export price of goods that have an import content. Productivity rises plus price falls due to import content will restrain any export price rises due to exchange rate adjustment. The government would have to ensure that this was happening by developing its economic strategy.

The amount of revenue accruing to the oil account would depend on the rate of expansion of oil exploration and exploitation. It may be in the interest of a Scottish government to slow down the oil flow beyond the currently envisaged levels. Oil may be discovered in English waters too.

It should therefore be clear from this case study that the economics of independence are far from certain from whichever side of the debate you look at them. Economic analysis can be applied to the arguments; it cannot settle the issues unambiguously.

REFERENCES

Wilfred Beckerman, *An Introduction to National Income Analysis*, Weidenfeld and Nicolson, London, 1968.

H. M. Begg, C. M. Lythe, R. Sorley (University of Dundee), *Expenditure in Scotland 1961–1971*, Scottish Academic Press, Edinburgh, 1975.

H. M. Begg, C. M. Lythe, R. Sorley, *Special Regional Assistance in Scotland*, Fraser of Allander Institute, University of Strathclyde, Research Monograph No. 3, Edinburgh, 1976.

John Firn (University of Glasgow), 'External Control and Regional Policy' in Gordon Brown (ed.), *The Red Paper on Scotland*, Edinburgh University Student Publications Board, Edinburgh, 1975, pp. 153–69.

T. L. Johnston, N. K. Buxton, D. Mair (Heriot-Watt University, Edinburgh), *Structure and Growth of the Scottish Economy*, William Collins, London, 1971.

Alexander G. Kemp (University of Aberdeen), *Taxation and the Profitability of North Sea Oil*, Fraser of Allander Institute, University of Strathclyde, Research Monograph No. 4, 1976.

Gavin Kennedy (University of Strathclyde), 'Defence Employment and Expenditure in Scotland, 1975', University of Strathclyde, Department of Economics, Mimeo, 1976a.

Gavin Kennedy, 'Scotland's Economy' in *The Radical Approach : Papers on an Independent Scotland*, Palingenesis Press, Edinburgh, 1976b.

Gavin Kennedy (with David Greenwood, University of Aberdeen), 'A Scottish Defence Budget' in D. I. MacKay (ed.), *Scotland 1980 : Economics of Self-government*, Q Press, Edinburgh, 1977.

Labour Party (Scottish Council), *Labour's Analysis of the Economics of Separatism*, Glasgow, 1976.

Derek Lee, *Regional Policy and the Location of Industry*, Heinemann Educational Books, London, 1973.

William Lever, 'Migrant Industry, Demand Linkage and the Multiplier: some paradoxes in regional development', University of Glasgow, Urban and Regional Studies, Discussion Papers, No. 10, May 1974.

D. I. MacKay, *North Sea Oil Through Speculative Glasses*, Fraser of Allander Institute, University of Strathclyde, Speculative Paper No. 4, 1976.

——(ed.), *Scotland 1980: Economics of Self-government*, Q Press, Edinburgh, 1977

——(Heriot-Watt University) and G. A. Mackay (University of Aberdeen), *The Political Economy of North Sea Oil*, Martin Robertson, London, 1975.

Gavin McCrone, *Scotland's Future: the economics of nationalism*, Blackwell, Oxford, 1969.

Tom McRae (University of Bradford), *North Sea Oil and the Scottish Economy*, Andrew Fletcher Society, Fletcher Paper No. 2, Edinburgh, 1976.

Royal Scottish Geographical Society, *Scotland and Oil*, Teachers Bulletin No. 5, Edinburgh, 1973.

Scottish Office, *The Scottish Economic Bulletin*, H.M.S.O., Edinburgh, quarterly series, No. 9, Winter 1976.

——*Scottish Abstract of Statistics*, H.M.S.O., Edinburgh, annual series.

David Simpson (University of Strathclyde), 'Scotland, England and North Sea Oil' in Gavin Kennedy (ed.), *The Radical Approach: Papers on an Independent Scotland*, Palingenesis Press, Edinburgh, 1976, pp. 60–3.

Christopher Smallwood (University of Edinburgh), 'Independence not worth the candle', *The Scotsman*, 7th November 1975 (also in Labour Party, Scottish Council, 1976).

——'The Economics of Independence', in *Our Changing Scotland*, edited by H. Drucker, Edinburgh University, Edinburgh, 1976.

Alan A. Tait (University of Strathclyde), *The Economics of Devolution: a knife-edge problem*, Fraser of Allander Institute, University of Strathclyde, Speculative Paper No. 2, 1975.

V. H. Woodward, *Regional Social Accounts for the United Kingdom*, National Institute of Economic and Social Research, Regional Papers, No. 1, Cambridge, 1970.

M. Yanovsky, *Anatomy of Social Accounting Systems*, Chapman and Hall, London, 1965.

QUESTIONS FOR DISCUSSION

1. To what extent can the innate characteristics of a regional economy be separated from the influence of the national economy on the region and how, therefore, can we be certain about the economics of separation?

2. Faced with a deficit on its revenue/expenditure account a government can either raise revenue by taxation or borrowing or reduce expenditure. What else might a Scottish government do if it wished to cover such a deficit (ignore oil revenues)?

3. Why is it necessary in regional social accounting to estimate domestic product rather than national product? How could Scotland's national product exceed her domestic product if exports equalled imports?

4. What caveats are necessary when using domestic product and domestic expenditure identities to estimate the trade balance? What new policies could a Scottish government pursue to improve its trade balance (ignoring oil revenues)?

5. Does external control of companies matter and if it does, what can be done about it?

6. How dependent is the economic viability of North Sea oil on the world price for oil?

7. In what sense are oil and independence 'not worth the candle'?

8. If Scotland's industrial structure is in decline and will continue to be so, come independence or continued Union, what can be done about it under (a) centralized regional policies (b) devolution and (c) independence?

9. If the exchange value of the British pound continues to fall, will this help Scottish industry? If the Scottish pound rises, will this help?

10. In what circumstances would oil not benefit a Scottish government? Given these circumstances what policies concerning oil should a government pursue?

11. Is the Simpson Plan for a joint oil account between Scotland and England workable?

12. To what extent can two countries who are major trading partners and both members of the European Economic Community pursue different macroeconomic policies?

13. Why might a Scottish government be interested in reducing the flow of oil below currently expected levels?

14. How could Scotland use any surplus sterling funds under the working of a joint account arrangement?

Savings in the United Kingdom

It is the purpose of this case study to indicate the nature of saving in the UK and to estimate the importance of saving to the UK economy. It reviews the policies discussed in the 1960s to raise the savings ratio and examines why in fact that ratio rose in the early 1970s despite escalating price inflation.

SAVING

The principal factors which influence the level of savings are usually held to be as follows:

1. *The level of income*. Saving is impossible until the level of income is sufficient to cover the basic necessities of life. As income increases, so does the ability to save. The rich man will spend a greater sum of money but a smaller proportion of his total income than a poor man. The same argument is true of society as a whole.

2. *Attitudes to saving*. Where thrift is regarded as a virtue, more will be saved. In the last century, hard work and general thriftiness were regarded as admirable characteristics, and this had considerable effect on economic growth of the period.

3. *Financial institutions*. In advanced economies there are many kinds of institutions for the safe deposit of savings. Commercial banks, savings banks, insurance companies, building societies, government securities and company shares are widely known, easily accessible and have the confidence of the people. The variety of institutions not only stimulates saving but also enables borrowers to obtain access to these savings.

4. *The rate of interest*. There is some controversy among economists over the influence of the rate of interest on the level of savings. One approach such as that of Böhm-Bawerk emphasizes the importance of time preference. Interest is a reward for the sacrifice of current consumption. Most people would probably prefer purchasing power now to the promise of purchasing power in the future. The stronger one's preference for present satisfaction over future satisfaction, the stronger is one's time preference. Interest may thus be regarded as a payment necessary to overcome people's time preference. If the choice is £100 now or £115 in one year's time and £15 is only just sufficient compensation for waiting, a rate of interest of 15 per cent is required to overcome time preference.

In an advanced economy however it is now conventional wisdom to doubt whether the rate of interest has a tremendous influence on the level of savings. High rates of interest may encourage some people with a strong time preference to start saving, and others already saving, to save more. Other factors, however, are also important. Habit plays an important part. Many people extol the virtues of thrift and others enjoy the feeling of security of some 'capital' behind them. The rate of interest will have little effect on this type of saving. Furthermore a considerable proportion of saving is contractual. The saver agrees to pay a fixed sum to an insurance company (the premium) or a fixed percentage of income for a super-annuation contribution. Variations in the rate of interest will therefore not affect existing contracts but they may of course influence future contracts. Many people save for a specific target, such as for the purchase of a car or a summer holiday. The rate of interest will have little effect on this motive for saving, although higher rates will tend to reduce the level of such saving since the required sum can be achieved more quickly.

In fact company saving accounts for nearly half the total saving in the UK. Firms save by retaining undistributed profits. The object may be to finance future investment programmes internally, or it may be to build up a reserve which can be used to even out the payment of dividends, adding to reserves in good years when profits are high and paying out from reserves when profits are low. The existence of business savings tends to stabilize the level of consumption against the effects of changes in income. When total incomes are rising, undistributed profits will tend to increase and consumption will rise by less than if all profits had been distributed. Alternatively, when total income is falling, the income of shareholders may be held constant by drawing from reserves and so consumption will fall that much less. Again company savings are unlikely to vary with changes in the rate of interest, since income in the form of interest is not the purpose of such saving.

The government also has an influence on part of total saving. When a government budgets for a surplus, that is when government revenue from taxation exceeds government expenditure, there is a form of compulsory saving by the public.

Keynes, in his *General Theory* asserted that it is 'a fundamental psychological rule of any modern community that, when its real income is increased, it will not increase its consumption by an equal absolute amount', and that 'as a rule . . . a greater proportion of income will be saved as real income increases'.[1] Much of the evidence which has since become available would tend to confirm Keynes' hypothesis but a study by S. Kuznets of national income data for the USA seemed to show that despite a substantial rise in income during the last half century, savings had not increased their share in national income.[2] In order to reconcile this finding about the long-term, with the apparent short-term behaviour of savings, a number of writers have suggested more sophisticated versions of the consumption function, notably Duesenberry, Milton Friedman, Modigliani and Brumberg.[3] These theories assume that not only current but past levels of income affect consumers' expenditure and also that the long-run propensity is for a constant proportion of income to be spent. Thus a rise in income takes time to have full effect, so that at first less than the normal proportion will be spent; but in the end only the same fraction of income will be spent as before.

WHO SAVES?

Some classes of the population tend to do most of the saving. In the early fifties, the largest savers were the self-employed, much of whose savings went direct into their own businesses. Next came the 'managerial and technical' group and then skilled manual workers. Clerical and sales staff, and unskilled manual workers appeared to save very little. The fifth of the population who were retired or unoccupied were, however, considerable dis-savers. Estimates of marginal propensity to save suggest that the marginal propensity of the self-employed in the 1950s was much higher than average and they saved a third or even a half of any increase in income. For managerial and technical groups, the marginal share of saving, though appreciable, was much less. For the retired, the rate at which they lived on past saving appeared unrelated to their current income.[4]

CHANGES IN THE LEVEL OF SAVINGS

There was a perceptible decline between 1961 and 1963 in the ratio of personal savings to personal disposable income (from 8·5 per cent to 7 per cent) and this had not recovered at all by 1967. Why should such a change take place? Does it matter in terms of the government? To take the second issue first, post-war governments have tried to both raise and keep stable the ratio of savings to personal disposable income. This has been effectively to mobilize resources to provide new finance for the economy as well as to curb and regulate personal consumption efficiently. The question of what causes changes in the level of savings is a complex one. The Radcliffe Committee Report in 1959 had announced: 'We have found no satisfactory explanation of the large changes that have taken place in the rate of private saving over the past ten years'.[5] The level and growth of personal disposable income, however, dominates the savings ratio. The pattern in the 1960s has periods of rapid growth in disposable income with high savings in the following year, as real consumption begins to fall back. Expansions of 1955, 1960 and 1963 were followed by hgh savings ratios in 1956, 1961 and 1964. It must be noted, however, that government curbs on consumer demand followed these years of expansion, and these would tend to encourage saving.

Taxation has some effect on the savings ratio. Some forms of taxation have more effect than others. Direct taxes on income have much more effect than others. Direct taxes on income have much more impact on the proportion of income saved than indirect taxes. Higher income groups tend to have the greatest propensity to save, so that any increase in tax on their incomes has a disproportionately sharp effect on the savings ratio. By international standards, in the 1960s, personal savings in Britain compared unfavourably. In the 1960s, the Japanese saved nearly a fifth of their disposable income and the Germans over a tenth. The British average was little more than a twentieth. Caution is however necessary in interpreting these figures: most of the divergencies are the result of different statistical methods, or of structural differences.

In Britain there is a large proportion of contractual saving through life assurance and pension funds. Between 1962 and 1966, the net increases in life assurance and superannuation schemes made up three-fifths of the total increase in savings. This does not necessarily imply any rise in savings as a whole since throughout the 1960s the personal sector switched from holding securities directly to holding them indirectly through funds such as these. A high rate of contractual savings allows savings to reach the capital market through specialized investors and thus the collection and distribution of funds is made more efficient. In addition contractual savings are fairly insulated from the effects of short-run fluctuations in income. This makes them more stable.[6]

TOO LITTLE SAVING: AN EXPLANATION

In an attempt to explain why Britain was at the bottom of the international savings league in the 1960s, David Lomax and Brian Reading argued that 'the lower level of personal savings in comparison with other countries, which is another way of describing the higher level of consumption, is not accidental, but a direct consequence of the ways in which our tax system differs from theirs, and that the disincentives to savings in this country have been increasing over time'.[7] It is interesting that this conclusion was in direct contrast with that written by Professor Hill in an earlier article in the same journal! Hill in his article, 'Too Much Consumption', in which he implied that increased taxation might strengthen the economy, said '. . . the experience of several other countries suggests . . . that the basic weakness of the UK economy may be that we have been consuming too much because we have not been taxed heavily enough'.[8]

Although international comparisons of savings and taxation are notoriously difficult, Table 3.1, based on OECD statistics, clearly demonstrated Britain's below par performance in personal saving, 4·8 per cent compared with the average 10·8 per cent for the other six countries in the table.

Table 3.1 Personal Savings, Incomes and Taxation

Country	Personal Savings as Proportion of Personal Disposable Income (%)	GNP per Head at 1963 Prices and Exchange Rates ($ in 1967)	Taxes on Household Incomes % of Total Taxation	% of GNP
	(a)	(b)	(c)	(d)
Netherlands	14·3	1,810	30·3	12·5
Switzerland	13·9	2,620	36·0	8·5
West Germany	12·6	2,030	23·3	9·5
France	9·2	2,190	11·3	5·2
Sweden	8·8	3,040	45·0	21·0
US	6·0	4,040	35·4	10·9
Average	10·8	2,620	30·2	11·8
UK	4·8	1,980	31·2	11·8

Source: D. Lomax and B. Reading, 'Too little saving', *National Westminster Bank Quarterly Review*, August 1969, p. 26.

Although income per head is fairly low (column (b)) it is above the level of the Netherlands (top of the table), while the United States, with the highest income, is next to Britain at the foot of the table. It is also clear from columns (c) and (d) that Britain's poor savings performance cannot be explained by total taxes on household incomes, since Britain collects an average amount of total taxation from incomes and takes an average proportion of GNP in this way. The real difference between British and other tax systems which is significant for savings was the severity of our direct tax system on higher levels of income and on the returns from savings.[9] This has been partly the result of policy but also the result of post-war inflation. The authors commented, 'It is a characteristic of any progressive tax, such as the British direct tax system, that it becomes more progressive as incomes rise – whether the rise is due to a real increase in income or reflects inflation.'[10] Lomax and Reading suggested that although action on savings would not be sufficient to cure all our economic ills, encouragement of savings along with other policies would lead to much improved demand management. The authors concluded that consumption behaviour is such that a government policy of drastically reducing consumption is not possible without such sharp tax increases that their adverse side effects would offset their beneficial effects. Steady growth of the public sector, rather than irregular acceleration is all that the economy can tolerate without balance of payments and inflation problems. Governments 'should adopt the objective of permitting a reasonably steady growth of real personal disposable income. . . . Reducing the marginal rates of direct taxation, especially on investment income, is a necessary part of encouraging savings.'[11]

In an article in the *Three Banks Review* a year earlier, Sir John Hicks had supported the contention that the low level of personal savings was perhaps at the root of Britain's economic problems. Since the early 1960s it had been impossible to improve the British economic growth rate without putting a strain on the balance of payments. Sir John stated 'A common failing of business management, when undertaking an expansion programme, is to make insufficient allowance for the requirement of working capital which it will entail. This, on the grand scale, is what has happened to the British economy.'[12] He then pointed out that to maintain production at a high level, a more or less proportionate increase in 'stock and work in progress' will be required to support it. Sir John compared the real growth rate of the British economy, that is growth rate at constant prices between 1958 and 1967, with the value of physical increase in stock and work in progress (*see* Table 3.2). He showed the physical increase

Table 3.2 United Kingdom: the National Residual

Year	Growth Rate (%)	Stock Accumulation (£m.)	Balance of payments on current account (£m.)
1958	−0·2	111	+347
1959	3·5	174	+149
1960	4·1	602	−258
1961	3·7	334	+ 5
1962	0·9	83	+127
1963	4·2	228	+116
1964	5·7	649	−402
1965	2·6	416	−110
1966	1·8	210	− 31
1967	1·1	125	−514

Source: Sir J. Hicks, 'Saving, investment and taxation: an international comparison', *Three Banks Review*, June 1968, p. 5.

valued at average prices for the year. This is to make it comparable with the third column, the balance of payments on current account. The second column clearly reflects the fluctuations in the first column. When one allows for the 'carry-over' of stock accumulation from one year to another, the correspondence is very close. The balance of payments on current account fluctuates in the opposite direction to stock accumulation except for 1967. This relationship again is to be expected. When the economy is 'stocking up', stocks which cannot be obtained at home must be imported; when the rate of stock accumulation is lower, the pressure on the balance of payments is less. Sir John takes stock accumulation and payments balance as alternative uses of national savings, which taken together, he calls the National Residual. A country with a large Residual would be in a very comfortable situation but if the Residual is small and remains so over a period of years, the country will be in trouble. The size of the British Residual may be calculated by adding the second and third columns in the Table. The resulting series shows no decisive trend until 1966 but when correction is made for real changes rather than money movements, there is a falling trend in the Residual. Even in the early 1960s the British Residual was insufficient. Hicks concluded that for the British economy to grow, it must have an adequate Residual. He did not suggest, however, that Britain should attempt a rate of investment in Fixed Capital Assets anything like that of the Germans. He distinguished between necessary and luxury investment (public and private), recommending that Britain should concentrate on investment in plant and equipment, building construction and vehicles which would have an immediate impact on productivity.

Sir John's article included two tables which are reproduced as Tables 3.3 and 3.4.

Table 3.3 Sources of Saving as Percentages of National Income

	U.K. (Private and Corporate Saving)	(Government Saving)	France (Private and Corporate Saving)	(Government Saving)	Germany (Private and Corporate Saving)	(Government Saving)
1960–61	11·8	0·6	11·6	4·8	14·3	10·3
1962–63	10·2	1·4	11·2	4·1	12·0	9·4
1964–65	12·2	2·5	10·6	5·8	13·6	8·5

Source: Hicks, op. cit., p. 15

Table 3.4 Personal Saving as Percentage of Personal Disposal Income

	U.K.	France	Germany
1960–61	5·5	7·8	13·7
1962–63	5·3	8·8	12·2
1964–65	6·0	8·9	13·9

Source: Hicks, op. cit., p. 19.

SUGGESTIONS TO IMPROVE THE LEVEL OF SAVINGS IN THE 1960s

In the 1960s it was clear that the level of personal savings was far below that of our major competitors. A number of suggestions were made towards the end of the decade in order to stimulate personal savings. Harold Wincott, writing in the *Financial Times* in November 1967, stressed the importance of encouraging personal savings in order to ensure the success of devaluation rather than further increases in taxation. He commented '. . . we have now reached the point where any further increase in taxation of either incomes or spending is largely if not entirely self-defeating, if only because people adjust their savings, rather than their living standards, to such increases'.[13] He examined five savings media: building societies, pension funds, life offices, unit trusts and national savings. One surprising fact he noted, was the way in which building societies had virtually doubled the net annual increase in shares and deposits outstanding in the years 1962–6 when savings as a whole were unimpressive. Mr Wincott did not believe that the reason was the 'income tax paid by the society' since many investors in building societies do not pay income tax at the standard rate on their marginal income. Pension funds were the next largest gatherers of savings. Savings through them are contractual, virtually involuntary, and although they have growth, their progress had not been sensational and Mr Wincott saw little prospect of further increase in the rate of growth. Life assurance was in a similar situation but it had not grown as fast as it might have done. In an article on contractual saving in a then recent issue of *Economic Trends*, Lawrence S. Berman, Chief Statistician at the Central Statistical Office, showed that the net increase in the funds of the life offices represented 3·2 per cent of personal disposable income in 1952, rose to 5·0 per cent of incomes in 1964, but then slipped back to 4·6 per cent in 1966.[14] The fastest-growing means of savings however was the unit trust, but in 1967 the unit trust investor was less keen to invest. In the first ten months of 1967 £61 million was invested compared with £94 million in the same period of 1966.

The National Savings Movement, however, had deteriorated from a plus of £357 million in 1964 to a minus of £30 million in 1966, although there was some sign of improvement in 1967. The main reason advanced by Wincott for the recovery was the outstanding contribution to National Savings by the Trustee Savings Banks. In Britain, Mr Wincott argued, a new attitude to savings was necessary. Wincott stated that if the British people could be persuaded 'to save a modestly higher proportion of their incomes, additional to their existing contractual savings, not only would we have avoided our crises but we could have kept taxation down, increased our productive investment and achieved a better spread of wealth'.[15]

There is the problem of providing incentives to increase savings. One interesting scheme was that prepared by Brian Reading in April 1968. His plan was for special three-year tax-free savings accounts. He estimated that personal spending would be reduced by up to £250 million a year. After three years, the savings (voluntarily deductive with PAYE) would be transferred into the Post Office or other forms of saving. Lionel Barras suggested that the total tax payable under Schedule E in any year of assessment be abated by 10 per cent of the aggregate investments made by the individual in recognized savings media (mainly National Savings Certificates and unit and investment trusts) with a limit on the relief of £25 in any year, with loss of the tax relief on premature sales.[16]

The Wider Share Ownership Council suggested 'thrift plans' such as those adopted in the USA where employees regularly subscribe to a trust for investment in approved media, plus shares in the company which employs them, which supplements employees' contributions, all contributions (up to 5 per cent of taxable income) being a charge for tax purposes. Withdrawal would be permitted after three years, provided that the person withdrawing is debarred from further participation for another three years.

The Confederation of British Industry also produced several ideas, mainly concerned with fixed interest media. The CBI suggested the Wider Share Ownership Council's ideas but envisaged also an alternative with a link with the cost-of-living index. High rates of interest or tax concessions should be conditional on the savings being frozen for a given period. The National Savings Committee advocated a three- to five-year 'lock-up' fixed interest medium with an interest rate well above current levels and a limit on the amounts which can be invested.

CONTRACTUAL SAVINGS SCHEMES

A Bow Group memorandum by Mr Tim Sainsbury suggested tax concessions for contractual savings on the lines of the CBI. It also suggested tax concessions on small amounts of investment income irrespective of source. A more interesting idea of Mr Sainsbury's was that the size of the tax incentive under a contractual savings scheme should vary with the state of the economy. This would be a much more popular regulator than the conventional tax ones, particularly if advertised with the slogan 'it pays to save now and spend later'.[17]

The CBI argued that few forms of saving offer sufficient return. 'The real return from saving in recent years, net of taxation, and the fall in the value of money, has been small and sometimes negative.'[18] In addition, the CBI pointed out that on many forms of National Savings, only tax relief on the interest prevents the real return being completely wiped out by inflation. In 1968, the total outstanding in National Savings increased by only £77 million, very different from the early 1960s when the total was increasing by £200–300 million a year.

Some of the proposers of contractual savings schemes wanted an anti-inflation device by linking up with a unit trust; others wanted such schemes to provide a higher return without competing directly with other media, by offering tax concessions on interest, or even on the principal;

others favoured schemes to aim at the small saver, offering a bonus at the end of the contractual period rather than a tax concession, or by imposing a ceiling on the amount that could be saved through it; and some liked schemes to be tied to saving for a specific purpose, such as house purchase. The Treasury until recently was of the view that any new savings scheme simply results in a switch of savings out of existing media, and does nothing to increase the *total* money saved. But in 1969 the government introduced the 'Save As You Earn' plan to be operated by the Department for National Savings, Trustee Savings banks, and building societies.

CHANGES IN THE PROPORTIONS OF PRIVATE AND PUBLIC SAVINGS 1960-70

In the June 1971 edition of the Treasury *Economic Progress Report*, some changes were noted in the five categories of savings. In 1970 the personal sector provided 26 per cent of total savings, companies 28 per cent, central government 34 per cent, public corporations 7 per cent and local authorities 4 per cent. Since 1960, the personal sector's share of savings, as a proportion of GNP has remained very steady ranging between 5·1 per cent and 6·3 per cent, with an average of 6·19 per cent. In the late 1950s, company savings accounted for about 55 per cent of all saving but had declined to 28 per cent in 1970. Public saving varied considerably, increasing from 16 per cent of total saving in 1960 to 25 per cent in 1965, 35 per cent in 1968 and 45 per cent in 1970. Within this total, the share of public corporations and local authorities had remained fairly steady. The central government varies its rate of saving according to not only the amount of investment it wishes to finance but also to the state of the economy as a whole. In the Budget speech in 1971, the Chancellor said that the government was 'pledged to encourage all forms of personal saving'.[19] The Budget provided a new £50,000 Premium Bond prize, increased bonuses on British Savings Bonds, a higher limit of £1,000 for individual holdings of National Savings Certificates, as well as various tax concessions to encourage savings. The limit on monthly contributions to 'Save As You Earn' was relaxed so that anyone over the age of 16 could save up to £40 per month, by deductions from pay, standing orders or in cash through the post office. After five years a person saving £1 per month would receive a tax-free bonus of £12 or, if the money is not withdrawn for another two years, £24.

SAVING AND INFLATION

Despite rapid rates of inflation between 1973 and 1975, the British saver went on saving, even though real interest rates were negative and the saver lost relatively by holding almost any financial asset. The British saver appeared to believe that inflation of over 25 per cent a year was a passing phase, not a permanent change in the economic climate, and he was willing to pay for security by the loss of part of the value of his savings. By lending at a return of 5–7 per cent, the saver allowed businesses to go on borrowing at 10 per cent or so. The negative real interest rates which savers accepted prevented both the financial system and the British economy from collapsing. If interest rates had risen to 25 per cent in line with rising prices, the financial institutions would have seen most of their assets destroyed. The financial crisis did not overcome many reputable and properly run institutions, but the secondary banking system was hard hit, along with speculative property companies and some ailing industrial and commercial companies. In the eighteen months to mid-1975 Britons with any savings lost a quarter of the real value of their personally held financial wealth. Lord Diamond's Royal Commission on the distribution of income and wealth estimated that the value of Britons' individually owned wealth exceeded £200 billion at the end of 1973. Physical assets such as houses and consumer durables were valued at £140 billion; total financial assets, such as bank deposits and ordinary shares, at £112 billion, against which there were an estimated £37 billion of personal financial liabilities. *The Economist* calculated that the £112 billion of financial assets fell to £86 billion at end-1973 prices, and at mid-1975 prices the loss increased from £26 billion to £35 billion.[20]

Domestic economic forecasting has been notoriously unreliable in recent years. One of the most important errors has been in forecasting private saving. People have saved much more, and spent correspondingly less, than the forecasters expected. One National Institute forecast for the UK put the future personal savings ratio as 11 per cent of disposable income, but admitted that the out-turn might well be 2 per cent higher or lower than that – a 20 per cent margin of error either way in terms of the sum actually saved. The Treasury in April 1975 was equally vague: 'Rapid inflation may be expected to have lessened the share of income saved, but the fall in asset values and a desire to have some readily access-ible funds may have been influences working in the appropriate direc-tion.'[21] The Treasury's remarks express doubts about all the received ideas about saving, which depend in one form or another on a relationship between saving and the level of, and changes in, mainly real income rather than money income. The Treasury was suggesting that savings behaviour might also be influenced by people's feelings about their stock of assets. However 'value of assets' is itself a vague term. It could mean stock market prices, house prices or a whole spectrum of assets revalued in real terms; saving and dis-saving cannot always be disentangled and different factors may explain why people want to build up their holdings of financial assets or do not wish to incur further financial liabilities.

THE LIQUIDITY-SAVINGS TRADE-OFF

One theory propounded by Mr John Forsyth, Chief Economist to the merchant bankers, Morgan Grenfell, is that savings are related to liquid assets and to income. Mr Forsyth's thesis is that the amount people save is largely determined by the ratio between their liquid assets and their disposable income. Put simply, it says that people spend more of their income when they have plenty of money already saved up in bank deposits, building society deposits, national savings and other liquid assets. When income rises, this stock of liquidity declines in relation to income unless it is built up out of current saving. People do not immediately restore their liquidity-income ratio but, when incomes rise, they work towards restoring it. Even more simply, a person is more likely to spend up to his full income if he has £500 in the bank than if he has only £100 in it. The idea is not only simple but also measurable and more important, it seems to work. A relationship measured from the relatively stable 1960s gives quite a good forecast of the actual level of savings in the eighteen months to September 1975 and a much better forecast than the purely income-determined relationship. Inflation has been accompanied by rising money incomes, by negative real interest rates, and a fall in the ratio of liquid assets to income. Mr Forsyth explains Britain's high saving ratio in 1974–5 as an attempt to restore this ratio to a more normal level. The relationship is displayed in the scatter diagram (Figure 3.1). The points show a marked clustering round one line rather than being evenly scattered over the whole diagram. The figures are quarterly covering a decade. Each point shows, on the vertical axis, the percentage of disposable income saved in a quarter: and on the horizontal axis, the ratio of liquid assets to disposable income in the *previous* quarter. (The time lag allows for the fact that people may not know what has happened to their cash balances until they receive a statement a little way in arrears, and more importantly, for the fact that it takes time to adjust spending habits.)

Quarterly figures provide a large number of observations but have the disadvantage of being subject to seasonal distortions such as Christmas and holiday spending. The liquid assets measured are net bank balances, deposits with building societies, finance houses and local authorities, national savings and tax reserve certificates. The diagram shows two very different periods. To the end of 1969 the points are bunched near the bottom right hand corner of the diagram: incomes and the ratio of incomes to liquid assets were very stable, and so too was the savings ratio. In the 1970s, the growth of incomes shot far ahead of the growth of liquid assets. The savings ratio rose as people found their assets dwindling in real terms. Yet it had been predicted quite recently that accelerating inflation would provoke a 'flight from money' a sharp *fall* in savings.

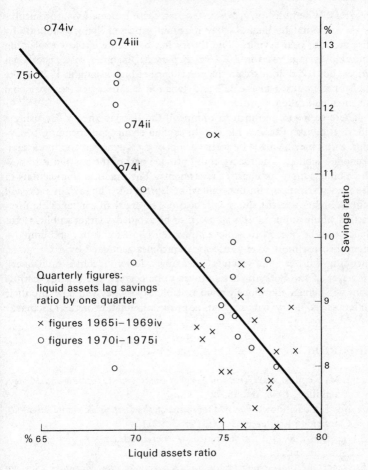

Figure 3.1 The Liquidity-Savings Trade-Off

Quarterly figures: liquid assets lag savings ratio by one quarter
x = figures 1969 i–1969 iv   o = figures 1970 i–1975 i
Source: J. Forsyth, 'Savings, inflation and recession', *Morgan Grenfell Economic Review*, 9 September 1975.

Large negative interest rates were supposed to discourage the holding of money-dominated assets. Saving however has *risen* and people have added to their liquid holdings. It is only the ratio of assets to income that has fallen.

The relationship works much better than ideas such as the Milton Friedman 'permanent income' hypothesis. This states that people have strong underlying expectations about their standard of living and its progress. When income grows faster than these expectations, the surplus is saved; if it falls behind, they maintain expected living standards by dipping into past savings. The theory has had some success explaining the high savings ratio in 1974 when personal incomes rose faster than prices, but it did not explain the persistence of high saving in 1975 or the high savings ratios in the US and Japan at a time when real personal incomes had fallen sharply.[22]

There seems to be much to commend the Forsyth theory. By using a stock ratio, assets against income, to explain changes in spending behaviour, a link may be made between the opposing Keynesian and monetarist economic schools. The theory could provide part of the answer as to how the money supply influences the economy. The practical implications of the theory are important but somewhat depressing. The savings ratio will remain higher and the slump will be more severe than conventional forecasters would suppose. If a slump is to be avoided a larger public sector deficit will be needed to achieve any given boost to output and employment, because more of any increase in incomes generated by extra public spending will leak into savings, meaning a lower 'incomes multiplier'. However, if the Forsyth thesis proves to be correct, the savings institutions will benefit enormously as an avalanche of money will flow into their coffers as people try to make good the ravages of inflation on their savings.[23]

REFERENCES

1. J. M. Keynes, *The General Theory of Employment, Interest and Money*, Macmillan, 1936, pp. 96–7.
2. See J. C. R. Dow, *The Management of the British Economy 1945–60*, Cambridge University Press, 1968, p. 271.
3. See Dow, *op. cit.*, for references to these authors.
4. Dow, *op. cit.*, p. 275.
5. *Report of the Committee on the Working of the Monetary System*, August 1959, Cmnd. 827.
6. F. Cairncross, 'Lower savings mean £560 million extra levy', *The Times*, 20 March 1968.
7. D. F. Lomax and B. Reading, 'Too little saving', *National Westminster Bank Quarterly Review*, August 1969, pp. 23–42.
8. T. Hill, 'Too much consumption', *National Westminster Bank Quarterly Review*, February 1969.
9. Lomax and Reading, *op. cit.*, p. 28.
10. *ibid.*, p. 29.
11. *ibid.*, p. 39.
12. Sir John Hicks, 'Saving, investment and taxation: an international comparison', *Three Banks Review*, June 1968, p. 3.

13. H. Wincott, 'A new campaign to boost personal savings', *Financial Times*, 28 November 1967.
14. L. S. Berman, 'A note on contractual saving in the United Kingdom', *Economic Trends*, Vol. 66, August 1967, p. ix.
15. H. Wincott, 'Sudden attack of common sense on savings', *Financial Times*, 18 June 1968.
16. *ibid.*
17. S. Brittan, 'A case for a savings regulator', *Financial Times*, 19 December 1968.
18. Cited in F. Cairncross, 'Making Britain Save', *The Times*, 24 March 1969.
19. D.E.A., *Economic Progress Report*, No. 16, June 1971, p. 2.
20. B. Reading, 'Who dunnit?' in Savings Survey in *The Economist*, 29 November 1975, p. 5.
21. Cited in A. Harris, 'Why people save in spite of inflation', *Financial Times*, 12 September 1975.
22. *ibid.*
23. 'Saving on a rainy day', *The Economist*, 13 September 1975, p. 91.

QUESTIONS FOR DISCUSSION

1. What are the principal factors which influence the level of savings?
2. Who are the main savers in Britain, and has the situation changed in recent years?
3. What causes changes in the level of savings?
4. What conclusions can be made from comparing savings in Britain, W. Germany and France?
5. How would you explain Britain's poor savings performance in the 1960s?
6. What suggestions have been made to improve the level of savings?
7. What changes may be noted in the various categories of savings during the period 1960–70?
8. What explanation may be offered for the British saver continuing to save even though real interest rates were negative during the period 1973–5?
9. In an article 'Watch that gap' in its issue of 22 November 1975 (pp. 73–4) *The Economist* said 'a new deflationary gap has now appeared, people everywhere are saving more than most economists had expected them to do'. What did it mean by the 'new deflationary gap' and what problems may be encountered in attempting to fill this gap?

Value Added Tax in the United Kingdom

This case study sets out to show the impact upon the UK economy of the recently adopted Value Added Tax. It concentrates upon why the UK, in common with most European countries adopted VAT; how the tax has been used as a macroeconomic regulator and how it has had both intentionally and unintentionally altered producer and consumer decisions.

In a modern economy the impact of a tax is greater than its pure revenue raising capabilities. The secondary effects of value added tax are found to be important considerations in addition to its primary revenue-raising role.

THE UNITED KINGDOM TAX REGIME AND VAT

It is important to be able to relate VAT to both the general structure of taxation in the United Kingdom and other sales taxes, of which it is one variety.

Taxes in the United Kingdom are levied upon personal and corporate income by Income Tax, Corporation Tax, and Capital Gains Tax where the sale of capital produces an increase in income in the form of a capital gain. Not only capital gains, but also the advantages to be derived from the ownership of capital, or wealth, are taxed, for example Capital Transfer Tax and Stamp Duty. The latter is levied upon documents used in transacting certain types of business, such as the buying and selling of company stocks and shares.

As shown in Tables 4.1 and 4.2 other equally important taxes are those upon consumption – indirect, or sales, taxes and excise duties. Social security contributions made each week jointly by the employer and employee can be regarded as taxes rather than just premiums payable to a 'state insurance scheme'. Lastly, and not shown in Table 4.1, local authorities are empowered to levy local rates based upon an estimate of property values in their area.

There are three major ways in which a sales tax can be levied, in all cases the formal incidence of the tax falls upon the consumer, persons in the production chain before him simply act as unpaid tax collectors.

1. To levy the tax at one point late on in the production and distribution chain, for example at the wholesale stage; this is a single-stage sales tax.

2. To tax the good or service each time it is transferred between persons in the production and distribution chain; this is a general, or cumulative, turnover tax.
3. To tax only value added at each stage less tax previously paid; this is a non cumulative value added tax.

Table 4.1 Central Government Revenue 1976–7 – Forecast £m

Inland revenue		
Income tax	17,045	
Surtax	30	
Corporation tax	2,650	
Capital gains tax	400	
Estate duty	70	
Capital transfer tax	212	
Stamp duties	293	
Total Inland Revenue		20,700
Customs and excise		
Value added tax	3,650	
Oil	2,025	
Tobacco	1,790	
Spirits, beer and wine	1,850	
Betting and gaming	295	
Car tax	190	
Other revenue duties	10	
Protective duties	555	
Agricultural levies	60	
Total Customs and Excise		10,425
Vehicle excise duties		835
Total Taxation		31,960
Miscellaneous receipts		1,237
Grand Total		33,197

Note: The forecast revenue was conditional on agreement being reached on a low pay limit.

Source: *Financial Statement and Budget Report 1976–77*

Table 4.2 Taxes as Percentage of GNP at Market Prices

		1974	1975
1	Income tax	10·9	13·4
2	Direct taxes*	15·8	16·5
3	Indirect taxes	13·8	13·6
4	Social security contributions	6·1	6·6
5	Income tax and s.s. contributions	17·0	20·0
6	Direct taxes and s.s. contributions	21·9	23·1
7	Total tax and s.s. contributions	35·6	36·7

*Taxes on income and capital, as defined in national accounts.

Source: A. Harris, 'Taxes analysed as GNP percentages', *Financial Times*, 29 April 1976.

Table 4.3 Comparative Operation of General Turnover Tax, Single Stage Tax, and Value Added Tax, with 10% Rate for All Three Taxes

	Value of Product Excluding Tax	General Turnover Tax*	Value Added Excluding Tax	Value Added Tax	Single Stage Tax
Manufacturing stage	100	10·00	100	10·00	–
Wholesale stage	125	13·50	25	2·50	–
Retail stage	200	22·35	75	7·50	20·00
Final value of product	200		200		
Tax on final value		45·85	20·00	20·00	20·00

*The general turnover tax has been imposed on the value at each stage as increased by the tax at the previous stage. Under a value added tax, this type of multiple taxation is avoided by a legal provision that the firm's accounts register purchases net of tax.
Source: C. K. Sullivan, *The Tax on Value Added*, Columbia University Press, 1965, p. 7.

As system (2) makes no allowance for previously paid tax it is, in part, a tax upon a tax. The EEC now operates a non-cumulative value added tax system to avoid this problem. Figure 4.1 shows the operation of such, and Table 4.3 illustrates clearly the differences between the three approaches.

If we assume that:

VA is value added
t is the tax rate
O is total current output
I is total current inputs

Then for purchases on current account, ignoring capital and stocks, value added will be equal to:

$$O-I \qquad (1)$$

By applying the tax rate t, tax liability (tVA) will be:

$$t(O-I) \qquad (2)$$

and O–I will be equal to wages plus profit.
If (2) is zero then no tax is due

greater than zero then tax is due

less than zero then a tax refund is due to the producer concerned.

The last situation is common as most countries, including the United Kingdom, employ 'zero rating'. This means that a producer can claim a refund of VAT paid on his inputs whilst his output is not subject to VAT, examples being food and exports. This should not be confused with 'being exempt', in which case businesses are not required to account for VAT and do not receive refunds of tax paid on their inputs.

We are now in a position to define the system of VAT employed in the UK. It is a 'multi-stage, non-cumulative, sales tax levied upon final private consumption (with some exceptions), of goods and services'.

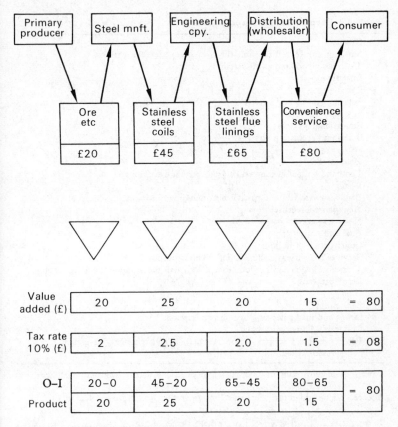

Figure 4.1 The VAT Process—An Example

Source: Adapted from: Exhibit One, D. Throop Smith, *Harvard Business Review*, November/December 1970, p. 78.

Note: All costs are fictitious.

The coverage of the tax is on the supply of all goods and services in the United Kingdom and on all imports of goods, except where the legislation makes specific provision to the contrary.

Businesses registered for VAT have to file quarterly accounts and forward the tax due to Customs and Excise no later than one month after the end of the collection period. Since it is possible for firms to receive tax credits, provision has been made to allow the filing of monthly accounts to expedite a company's cash flow.

Table 4.4 below gives details of exempt and zero-rated goods at the introduction of VAT, April 1973.

Table 4.4 Exempt and Zero-rated Categories

Exempt:
Small businesses with taxable turnover up to £5,000 a year
Transactions in land (with certain exceptions)
Insurance
Postal services
Betting, gaming and lotteries
Financial services
Educational services
Burial and cremation services

Zero-rated:
Food and animal feeding stuffs (with certain exceptions)
Water
Books, newspapers and periodicals (including music, maps, charts, etc.)
Newspaper advertisements
News services
Fuel and power
Construction of building, etc.
Services to overseas traders or for overseas purposes
Transport goods and services (except for small boats, motor cars, cycles, etc.)
Large caravans
Gold
Bank notes
Drugs and medicines supplied on prescription
Children's clothes and shoes
Foods previously subject to purchase tax, i.e. confectionery, ice-cream, soft drinks, etc.

Note: The zero-rating of food, coal, gas, electricity, fares, drugs and medicines is to avoid a regressive tax.
Source: 'Value added tax', *Economic Progress Report* No. 28, June 1972, p. 2.

The adoption of VAT by the United Kingdom was influenced by three factors:

1. membership of the EEC necessitated harmonization of indirect tax regimes;
2. the efficiency of Purchase Tax was beginning to be questioned and practical weaknesses likely to lead to a misallocation of resources were becoming evident;
3. several economists claimed that VAT was superior to other forms of indirect taxation and therefore should be seriously considered on its own merits.

Taking the last point first the following claims, and counter claims, have been made about VAT.

1. It taxes only value added and thus is an improvement over cascade taxes.
2. Evasion of tax payments is difficult since in order to gain a tax refund one needs to be able to produce a sales receipt, thus all transactions should be recorded. However, the administrative burden of VAT is high due to its being collected in stages. Although the percentage costs of collection for Customs and Excise are relatively low, the opportunity cost of collection in terms of leisure and other uses for the money spent to provide VAT accounts can be extensive. The smaller a trader is, the less sophisticated his accounting procedures might be and the costs of VAT calculation might be high.
3. Advocates of VAT argue that since the tax is rebated on exports and levied on imports it will favourably affect the balance of payments.
4. Most VAT systems employ a low rate applied over a very wide tax base. This can be advantageous as it reduces the number of goods and services not passing through the tax point. (Single stage retail taxes only affect goods passing through the retail stage.)
5. Indirect taxes are regressive as they fall on consumption which varies inversely with one's income level. Items forming a substantial percentage of low-income budgets are often zero-rated to offset this.
6. As VAT is a tax upon consumption, providing that demand is price-elastic around the pre-tax equilibrium, it would encourage saving, and this would be translated into investment in the Keynesian macro model.
7. A well-constructed tax regime should match up to certain criteria. Adam Smith's 'Canons of Taxation' were an early attempt to provide such criteria.[1] One such criterion is neutrality. Taxation systems can attempt to be as neutral as possible in their effect upon the distribution and use of resources in the economy.

   The price mechanism achieves an optimal allocation of resources by means of price signals which reflect both consumer preferences and producer costs. Price differentials reflect differences in production costs and consumer preferences. When a tax is introduced, the price of the good no longer reflects the true resource cost of production. One might therefore aim to minimize this distortion (represented by the loss of consumer and producer surpluses). The easiest way is to employ a broad-based tax, covering all goods and services at a single rate. Thus a VAT could be more neutral than a selective sales tax.
8. As VAT is a broad-based tax, over the years people have looked at the feasibility of reducing the direct tax burden by raising a higher percentage of revenue through indirect taxation. This becomes

particularly inviting if high marginal rates of direct taxation are felt to be discouraging work effort or profit-making. It is often claimed that indirect taxation is less inclined to produce a disincentive effect. It is a tax on what the consumer takes out of the economy, rather than a tax on what he puts into the productive process.

The countries forming the EEC adopted VAT as a response to problems that they then faced, or would face, after forming the community. France and Germany had cascade type sales taxes and the adoption of VAT eliminated a major distortion. The previous system had encouraged firms to integrate vertically thus reducing inter-firm transactions with a consequent lowering of their tax bill. Likewise specialization was penalized. France had a rudimentary VAT system by the early 50s, Germany adopted it in 1968. Both countries had had to make many arbitrary decisions about tax liabilities in the era of the cascade tax.

It is common practice to export goods tax-free with the country of destination levying the national tax upon imports. If exports were not treated like this, not only would they not be price-competitive but they would be taxed twice. It is technically difficult to calculate the total tax component under a cascade regime, and Governments had to resort to making average rebates. Under a VAT regime, by zero-rating exports, all previous inputs of the tax can be clearly identified and remitted.

Lastly the free movement of goods within a customs union on a fair basis, that is, reflecting the differing costs of production in each member country, can only be achieved if tax rates are harmonized. Otherwise the removal of political boundaries is offset by the remaining fiscal boundaries.

So it was eminently sensible for the United Kingdom to adopt VAT due to our impending membership of the EEC. Even if we had not wished to become a member, by 1972 problems with the existing system of purchase tax were becoming apparent. Although in 1964, the then Chancellor, Mr Maudling, was able to state:

> . . . in this country the purchase tax is superior as a method of taxation to the Value Added turnover tax, and there is no advantage either to exports or to the economy generally in switching over from Purchase Tax to to VAT.[2]

by the time of the Green Paper on VAT the Government was arguing that:

> The existing pattern of indirect taxation in this country is open to the objection that it is selective and is based on too narrow a range of expenditure.[3]

The NEDO Report of 1971 calculated that 93 per cent of indirect tax revenue (including duties) fell upon items that made up only 47 per cent of consumer spending.[4] Not only was this highly narrow base regressive with respect to items such as tobacco and alcohol, it adversely affected the stability of certain industries. Purchase tax and duty changes were used to regulate demand in the economy and their impact fell heavily on a limited number of industries such as motor vehicle assembly, violent cyclical fluctuations being caused in their sales and investment patterns. Neutrality was further transgressed by numerous rates and changes. In 1971 tax rates varied between 11·25 per cent and 45 per cent, maximum rates had varied between 25 per cent and 125 per cent, minimum rates 5 per cent to $33\frac{1}{2}$ per cent. The single-rate VAT replaced purchase tax which had had these distorting effects.

VAT AS A MACROECONOMIC REGULATOR

VAT has thus been adopted by many countries as an indirect tax and is levied on a wide variety of goods; as such it is part of the fiscal policy that a government may use in trying to achieve macroeconomic objectives. Fiscal policy arises out of the control government has over its revenue and expenditure.

Most taxes were originally introduced to pay for government expenditure, either generally or for specific purposes; for example, the National Insurance funds in the United Kingdom are supposed to pay for National Insurance benefits, though there is in fact a contribution from general tax revenue. The use of the various taxes and expenditures as instruments of fiscal policy was increasingly developed in line with Keynesian ideas during and after the Second World War. In the post-war period, new taxes have been introduced as much for their use as instruments of economic management as for their revenue earning capacity. Thus VAT was introduced partly to compensate for the anomalies experienced under purchase tax with its numerous rates and changes in rates. As a broad-based indirect tax, VAT in theory provides an improved macroeconomic instrument of control.

In simple Keynesian terms of national income determination, taxation (direct and indirect) is one form of withdrawal from the circular flow of income.

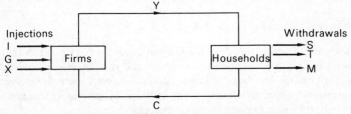

Figure 4.2 The Circular Flow of Income

Basically the theory uses the six aggregates of investment (I), savings (S), exports (X), imports (M), government expenditure (G), and taxation (T), and groups the injections I, G, and X and the withdrawals S, T and M to arrive at the equation:

$$I+G+X = S+T+M$$

This is both an ex ante and ex post statement. Ex post because injections in any year must equal withdrawals in any year. Ex ante because if planned (i.e. intended) injections equal planned withdrawals for the future year, there is equilibrium in the GNP. Thus, all the actual aggregates in the future year will turn out to be as planned. It is in this latter sense, of ex ante behaviour, that governments are most concerned. Until recently the overall aim of macroeconomic policy might crudely be summarized as allowing the planned expansion of aggregate demand in line with the expected expansion of aggregate supply potential. The riders must be added that over time, the balance of payments (X–M) and the budget balance (G–T) should be in equilibrium too.

Putting the statistics of the United Kingdom for 1975 into this aggregate form, Table 4.5 can be built up.

Table 4.5 United Kingdom Economy 1975, ex post figures (£m.)

Injections			Withdrawals			Balance	
Investment	(I)	13,000	Savings	(S)	21,300	(I–S)	− 8,300
Exports	(X)	19,000	Imports	(M)	20,700	(X–M)	− 1,700
Government Expenditure	(G)	44,000	Taxation	(T)	34,000	(G–T)	+10,000
		76,000			76,000		Nil

Source: B. Hodgkinson, 'General View', *British Economy Survey*, Spring 1976, p.2.

Note that there is no tendency for each of the individual items from the circular flow of income to balance each other. Thus,

$$S \neq I$$
$$M \neq X$$
$$T \neq G$$

But overall $$I+X+G = S+M+T$$

The figures describe the United Kingdom economy in 1975 when there was a large public sector deficit on current and capital account, and this was matched by the large amount by which savings exceeded private investment (public investment being included in government expenditure) and by which imports exceeded exports.

Taxation then is one part of the overall economic strategy that a government may pursue. In principle the Keynesian analysis offers clear-cut policy recommendations. If aggregate demand is projected to be less than full-employment aggregate supply for the coming year, the Chancellor of the Exchequer should adopt an expansionist policy-cutting taxes and hence increasing personal disposable income and consumption, or increasing government expenditure and so on. If aggregate demand is projected to be more than full-employment aggregate supply for the coming year, the Chancellor should adopt a deflationary policy – particularly increasing taxes and cutting government spending. Taxation then is a fiscal instrument that can be used for achieving short-term objectives particularly those of full employment and price stability. Other measures of a long-term nature may be necessary to deal with such problems as the distribution of income and wealth, regional disparities and declining industrial sectors leading to fundamental balance of payments disequilibria. Even in the short term, it must be remembered that fiscal policy is only one aspect of economic management: monetary and credit policy, exchange rate changes, direct control (prices and incomes policies) and institutional change are other tools of economic management.

When VAT was introduced in 1973 it was a single-rate tax at 10 per cent, though there was provision to set the starting level elsewhere within the range $7\frac{1}{2}$ per cent to $12\frac{1}{2}$ per cent. For the purposes of economic management, the Finance Bill included a regulator power to change the VAT rates between Budgets by Treasury Order by up to 20 per cent of the rate for the time being in force. This was to apply to VAT generally including cars, but not the new car tax of 1973. To the extent that differing countries have differing taxation rates then the introduction of VAT was expected to have a possibly beneficial effect on the balance of trade. The reason for the zero rating of goods was that although VAT is less distorting in its effects on prices than purchase tax and selective employment tax, it was felt that a general tax on consumer expenditure was regressive and discriminated against those on lower incomes. Thus a number of items were initially, and have continued to be, zero-rated. The period since 1973 has not been an easy one for the United Kingdom as it has faced the problem of 'stagflation' – stagnating output and rising unemployment combined with a price inflation that began to accelerate to well over 20 per cent per annum. The balance of payments has been persistently in deficit and the government's public sector deficit, and so the public sector borrowing requirement, has been as high as the previously presented figures indicate.

A succession of budgets have been introduced with various changes in the rates and coverage of VAT. Table 4.6 indicates the main changes and the overall economic package.

VAT has thus been extensively used as a short-term fiscal instrument, the July 1974 measures being aimed at directly affecting the retail price index

(RPI); the November 1974 measures aiming at cutting demand for petrol; the April 1975 measures aiming at cutting consumption expenditure.

Table 4.6 Changes in VAT and Economic Policy

April 1973	VAT Changes:	10% Basic rate; zero rating for food, newspapers, books, new houses, fuel and fares, etc. Exemption for small traders, rents, transactions in land and building, etc.
	Economic Package:	VAT replaced Purchase Tax and Selective Employment Tax; part of Tax Reform and European Tax Harmonization. Total taxation reduction of £120m.: expansionary budget aiming at 5% growth rate.
April 1974	VAT Changes:	10% Basic rate extended to petrol and derv., confectionery, soft drinks, ice-cream, crisps, etc. Will raise extra £290m. in full year.
	Economic Package:	Total taxation increase of £1378m. neutral/slight reduction in aggregate demand. Inflation and BOP becoming a problem.
July 1974	VAT Changes:	Basic rate reduced to 8%. Will cost £510m. in a full year.
	Economic Package:	Package aimed at directly lowering inflation rate via VAT cuts, rent/rate rebates, food subsidies, domestic rate relief, R.E.P. increase: these measures all affect the rate of domestic price rises.
November 1974	VAT Changes:	Rate on petrol (not derv.) raised to 25% increases VAT contribution by £200m.
	Economic Package:	Mildly expansionary. Tax reduction of £790m. Relief on stock appreciation, Price Code relaxations. Aimed to relieve financial pressure on firms and shift resources to exports and investment. VAT rise will encourage economy by private motorist; firms can reclaim VAT they pay.
April 1975	VAT Changes:	Basic rate remains 8%. 25% rate extended to less essential goods and services: domestic electrical appliances (other than cookers and heaters), radios, TV sets, hi-fi and similar equipment, certain boats, aircraft and caravans, cameras, binoculars, furs and jewellery, will raise revenue by £325m. in full year.
	Economic Package:	Total taxation increased by £1251m. Aimed to cut private consumption, continue movement to exports and investment to rectify balance of payments problem and build up industrial base.

| April 1976 | VAT Changes: | Higher rate of 25% reduced to 12½%. 8% Basic rate remains. |
| | Economic Package: | Aimed to be neutral in financial, tax and demand terms. Various measures to help industry and continue pay policy, such as tax relief or stock appreciation continued. |

Note: For a fuller table linking budgetary changes to overall industrial and economic policy, see *Economic Progress Report* No. 75, June 1976.
Source: extracted from various *Economic Progress Reports*.

The effects of VAT changes on the equilibrium level of national income are in theory easy to calculate using the multiplier, considering the stages in the multiplier process, and given an initial increase in GDP of £100 million (Table 4.7).

Table 4.7

	£m
1. 1st round increase in GDP	100
2. Increase in personal income	82
3. Increase in personal disposable income	56
4. Increase (after time lag) in consumers' expenditure at market prices	50
5. Increase in consumers' expenditure at factor cost	41
6. Increase in domestically produced consumption at factor cost (equals second round increase in G.D.P.):	31

$$\text{Hence multiplier} = \frac{1}{1-mpc} = \frac{1}{1-0.31} = 1.449$$

Source: A. R. Prest, D. J. Coppock, *The UK Economy: A Manual of Applied Economies* Weidenfeld & Nicolson, 1976, p. 28.

VAT affects line 5 in that higher rates of VAT will lower consumer expenditure at factor cost. The additional revenue generated (as estimated by the Board of Customs and Excise) will be multiplied by the multiplier derived from lines 5 and 6. Thus, given a tax multiplier of 1·5, an increase in VAT rates designed to raise an extra £300 million per year will lower GDP by £450 million.

The danger of this analysis is that it is too neat and logical. Economic policy suffers from a number of defects. The first is the problem of forecasting where the economy will be in the coming year, or years. If this is incorrect, budgetary changes based on such forecasts, may well exacerbate a situation. Secondly, it is not easy to calculate a tax multiplier as changes in indirect taxation invariably lead to differential changes in prices. The taxed goods go up in price whereas other prices are unchanged. Elementary economics suggests that there will then be substitution effects as well as income effects. It is really quite a complicated task to work out the effects of a tax change on consumers' spending on different articles and the revenue from the tax change. An important feature of estimates of tax change is that what appear severe changes in taxation may have quite small effects on the economy. Thirdly, there are time lags in the operation of VAT changes. For example, it has been estimated by Hopkin and Godley that it can take over two years for the *full* effect of a tax change to work through the economy.[5] In short-term demand management this limits the effectiveness of VAT, or any tax adjustments.

It is also true that economic theory has competing views on the causes and hence prescriptions for certain economic ills, for example inflation, and this does not make economic policy easier. Economic behaviour itself alters over time and VAT has been subject to a peculiar problem that will no doubt continue in coming years; the attempts by consumers to anticipate changes in the Budget, prior to actual Budget day, and to alter purchases accordingly. In the main, this has taken the form of anticipating VAT rises and buying the goods concerned before such rises become effective. This occurred at the introduction of VAT in Spring 1973, before the April 1975 Budget and is occurring at the time of writing prior to an expected December 1976 Budget. This anticipation, or 'beat the Budget' rush, in April 1975 meant that an exaggerated cyclical pattern of sales developed for luxury items. With television sets, April 1975 deliveries of monochrome were 28 per cent up on April 1974; deliveries of colour were 4 per cent up on April 1974. The April boom was then followed by a May collapse.

One final macroeconomic effect of VAT is the so-called VAT-flation. The retail prices index is composed of a number of items on which VAT is levied. Changes on VAT rates will thus have a direct effect upon the RPI. It was estimated that the introduction of VAT in April 1973 increased the RPI by several per cent. Similarly the July 1974 Budget measures cutting the standard rate to 8 per cent were designed to stabilize the RPI at a time of accelerating inflation. Other countries too have used VAT as a means to moderate inflation, e.g. France in January 1973 reduced its standard rate of VAT from 23 to 20 per cent, the intermediate rate from 7·5 to 7 per cent and the fresh pastry rate from 17·6 to 7 per cent.

CONTEMPORARY PROBLEMS

VAT has now been in operation for nearly four years in the United Kingdom, and in different forms for some time longer in other European countries. Experience has not diminished debate about the benefits of a value added tax but seems to have intensified it. A number of problems have been found in its operation.

At the introduction of VAT, British planners were convinced that VAT was a simple, administratively efficient tax to implement. Study of other countries systems showed that there would be enormous administrative advantages in keeping British tax free of the network of borderlines, detailed definitions and anomalies that inevitably enmeshes a multi-rate system (and had notably enmeshed the multi-rate purchase tax). The decision to have a single rate of tax was made also in Denmark.

The advent of multi-rates has meant a renewal of the old game of spotting tax anomalies. Considerable confusion and anomaly has arisen over a number of issues. One has been the definitional problems of which goods fall into the various categories.

In Spring 1975 Spanish guitars were taxed at 8 per cent, electric guitars at 25 per cent; records at 8 per cent, record players at 25 per cent, and so on. This is hardly a recognition of Adam Smith's principle that taxes should not be arbitrary. A further problem has been that servicing and parts for 8 per cent goods will be taxed at 8 per cent, but if the goods bear a higher rate then servicing and parts bear the higher rate too. Similarly the items entering the 'less essential goods' category, which bore the 25 per cent rate, were subject to some criticism. There may be support for the view that freezers and dishwashers are not among life's basic needs, but fridges, washing machines and vacuum cleaners were also placed among the 'less essential'. Multi-rates have brought back wrangling and confusion for producer and consumer.

The originally hoped-for simple tax has been replaced by the multi-rate system, as a single rate gave the Chancellor little flexibility in the management of the economy. With multi-rates, the Chancellor can theoretically control demand more easily and equitably by imposing higher taxes on luxury consumer goods while reducing the tax on essential items. However it still remains true that 'too many firms had underestimated the recording aspects of the tax, and the provision of the statistical information – together with the difficulties of interpretation have proved to be a heavy and expensive administrative burden'.[6]

The initial administrative burden for firms, particularly small firms, was difficult enough given the range of new taxes introduced in the 1970s; however, industry's case against the multiplicity of rates is based not on any real inability to cope (though some small businesses do find it difficult) but on the cost and inconvenience of having to do so. The move to multiple rates means that industry has had to face the prospect of frequent switching of rates, and of products from one rate to another, with the consequent disruption in the pattern of demand and hence production. This is particularly the case with price-elastic luxury goods. The European situation places the United Kingdom still in a reasonably manageable position, with two positive rates, a zero rate and an exempt category. European rates are shown in Table 4.8.

The issue of a uniform VAT rate in the United Kingdom has now become a political one as the Conservative party proposes a single rate of VAT and the simplification of the administration.

Table 4.8 Selected European VAT Rates at May 1975

Country			Rates as % of Prices before VAT
United Kingdom	exempt	zero-rated	8, 25
Belgium	exempt	zero-rated	6, 14, 18, 25
Italy	exempt	zero-rated	6, 15, 30
France	exempt	zero-rated	7, 17·6, 20, 33$\frac{1}{3}$
Republic of Ireland	exempt	zero-rated	6$\frac{3}{4}$, 11$\frac{1}{9}$, 19$\frac{1}{2}$, 36$\frac{3}{4}$

The question of the administrative efficiency of collecting VAT has also come up for scrutiny, on two counts. Firstly the numbers of taxmen employed on VAT alone have risen sharply in the last four years. Table 4.9 indicates this and includes estimates of further staff needed as given in 'a confidential' Report by a joint Customs and Excise and Civil Service Union working party, cited by the *Financial Times*.

Table 4.9

		Tax operative	No. of taxmen involved
	1973	Purchase Tax	2,000
April	1973	VAT = Staff needed[1]	8,000
May	1975	VAT	10,500
May	1976	VAT	11,600
July	1976[2]	VAT	13,270
July	1976[3]	VAT	14,270

Notes: 1. 'On best assumptions' (few of which were accurately fulfilled), *see* D. C. L. Johnstone, 'The VAT in the UK: some of the administrative problems of its introduction' in International Tax Conference, Singapore, 1974.
2. From joint report; numbers needed to 'maintain the present standard of administration, as given in D. Churchill, '£134m. VAT evasions reported', *Financial Times*, 8th July 1976.
3. From joint report; number needed in addition to 2 to reduce present level of evasion.

The increased number of staff involved is, in part, due to the extensive coverage of VAT. Purchase tax in 1973 was collected from 74,000 registered taxpayers. The number of taxpayers registered for VAT was expected to exceed 1 million. In 1975 the actual number of registered taxpayers was 1,223,800. Staff numbers have risen less than the increase in taxpayers. However revenue collected has not risen in line with the increase in staff numbers. In 1973, the last year of purchase tax, £1·4 billion was raised. In fiscal 1975, £2·5 billion was raised from VAT (£1·9 billion in 1973 real terms). Efficiency of collection, measured by real revenue raised per taxman, has declined.

The problem of evasion has become more apparent too, particularly where small firms and retailers are involved. Possible undeclaration rises as the complexity of the system increases. For example:

July 1975[1]	estimated £35–40m. lost
January 1976[2]	estimated £134m. found owing
	estimated £31m. expected to be lost permanently

Notes: 1. Mr R. Radford, chairman of the Customs and Excise, evidence to the
Accounts Committee, is reported in D. Churchill, *op. cit.*
2. From joint report of January 1976, also in Churchill, *op. cit.*

With the increase in evasion has come the difficulty of checking on
suspected evasion. From April 1973 to July 1976, 343 search warrants
were issued for 152 investigations into suspected fraud. Of these 326
produced evidence of offences leading to recovery of over £3 million. Yet
the number of search warrants per registered taxpayer per year is very
low, and the revenue recovered accounts for only half a per cent of the
£2·5 billion total. Nevertheless, the use of break-in powers by the
Customs and Excise has aroused some concern on the grounds of civil
liberties. It is certainly a defect in its administrative efficiency.

The move to tax harmonization, within the EEC, has proved to be slow
and arduous. Mr Henri Simonet said in March 1975 that there was no
chance of an agreement on the Sixth directive (to harmonize taxes) in the
forseeable future. The original hope of VAT being applied on the same
goods and at the same rate throughout the EEC has been abandoned. In
October 1976, the EEC Commission came up with proposals for gradual
alignment of tax rules and for using VAT as a revenue source for the EEC
itself. It was hoped that the alignment of rates and goods could be
achieved by 1978, so that a national 1 per cent VAT rate across the EEC
could be contributed by each national Treasury from its own national VAT
revenue. Problems of alignment have centred on various technical differences between national systems and on exemption rules in such systems.
Further meetings of the Fiscal Council are due to try and resolve the
issues outstanding.

CONCLUSIONS

In many respects the conclusions to this case study are negative, in that
the reasons put forward for VAT's adoption in the United Kingdom have
been found to be wanting. European tax harmonization, in the sense of
common VAT rates on common goods, is not much nearer than in 1973.
Limited progress has been made in using VAT as a revenue source for the
EEC but not as part of tax harmonization. The simplicity of VAT as it
appeared in 1973 when a single rate obtained, has given way to a multi-
rate system. The micro-economic effects and anomalies of purchase tax,
which gave way to VAT, seem to have carried on and bedevilled the
operation of the new tax. Far from proving to be an administratively easy
tax to collect, the rise in number of taxmen and of evasion, indicate that

VAT is not so simple to collect as at first thought. The use of VAT as a macroeconomic tool was seen to be fraught with difficulties, though here it did offer more flexibility than purchase tax had done.

In favour of VAT is the fact that it is undoubtedly a European tax. The European experience is that VAT has removed some of the inequities of cascade taxes which encouraged vertical integration of companies. The United Kingdom experience is that VAT is not substantially better or worse than the old purchase tax system. VAT could well be improved by less frequent changes in rates and product groupings, though this would run counter to demand management needs; the possible reintroduction of a single rate if accompanied by a restructuring of direct taxation; an increase in the exempt traders limit and the possibility of simplifying VAT returns and calculations. However, given that many commentators see direct taxation as having reached a maximum, then an increase in indirect taxation, and so in VAT, is the only method of increasing government revenue. VAT is with us for some time to come.

REFERENCES

1. Most basic textbooks refer to these Canons. C. M. Allan, *The Theory of Taxation*, Penguin, 1971, Chapter 3, updates and extends these.
2. Hansard No. 620, col. 249, 14 April 1964.
3. *Value Added Tax*, Green Paper, Cmnd 4621, 1971, p. 3.
4. National Economic Development Office, *VAT*, 1971.
5. W. A. B. Hopkin and W. A. H. Godley, 'An Analysis of Tax change', *National Institute Economic Review*, No. 32, May 1965.
6. D. F. Bailey, 'VAT: The Role of Customs and Excise', *Company Accountant*, May 1974.

QUESTIONS FOR DISCUSSION

1. Would a producer prefer to have the goods he produces zero-rated, or be exempt, and why?
2. Why did European countries abandon cascade type taxes?
3. Why should the EEC want a uniform system of indirect taxation?
4. For what reasons were multi-rates of VAT introduced in the UK?
5. What are the implications for demand management of using direct or indirect tax changes?
6· How efficient in collection is VAT compared to purchase tax?
7. What would be the effects of replacing the zero rate on food by a VAT rate of 8 per cent?
8. What changes in yield and coverage of VAT might you expect to take place in the coming decade?

9. Draw a diagram to illustrate the change in consumer and producer surplus caused by an increase in VAT on a product. How does elasticity affect these changes and revenue raised?

10. Why does the pattern of indirect taxation affect the income distribution in an economy?

Economic Growth and Industrial Fluctuations in the United Kingdom and West Germany in the Last Two Decades

This case study seeks to accomplish two tasks – firstly to compare the UK growth performance with that of West Germany over the last two decades; secondly it investigates one possible reason for the differences in performance recognized – the degree of industrial fluctuation in each country and the impact of that fluctuation upon economic growth. The first task however is to provide a definition of economic growth and to give an overview of all possible contributants to economic growth, for it must be stressed that the forces acting upon growth are many and varied. The fact that this study concentrates upon the connection between industrial fluctuation and growth must not lead the reader to lose sight of these other forces.

THE MEANING AND MEASUREMENT OF ECONOMIC GROWTH

A survey of the literature reveals that economic growth is generally taken to be an increase in real output of the economy over time. Output figures are expressed in real terms so as to exclude increases in value which are brought about by price rises rather than by physical changes in output.

The increase in output is usually expressed as an annual percentage change. Figures indicating the growth rate of real output are obtainable from each country's national income accounts and are given by the rate of change in Real Gross National Product (RGNP). If particular importance is placed upon growth as an indicator of changes in the standard of living, then most economists would prefer to employ growth rates in national product per capita or, if emphasis is placed upon productivity growth, the growth of real national product per employed person is a more appropriate indicator. For the purpose of this study annual growth rates of real gross national product are utilized.

Such an indicator of economic growth has encountered criticism on two grounds.[1] It has been doubted that a phenomenon as complex as growth can be accurately portrayed by any statistic as simple as an annual per-

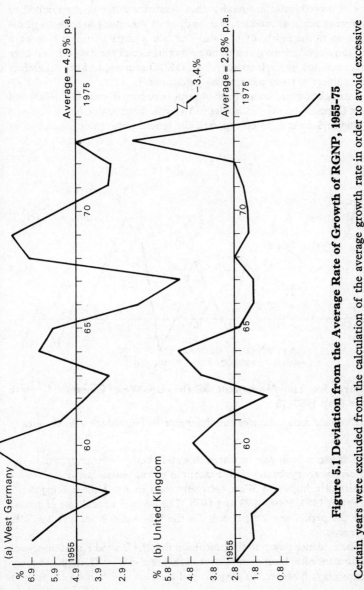

Figure 5.1 Deviation from the Average Rate of Growth of RGNP, 1955-75

Certain years were excluded from the calculation of the average growth rate in order to avoid excessive distortion, e.g. the 12% rate of growth for W. Germany in 1955.

Source: National Accounts of the O.E.C.D. countries, various years, O.E.C.D., Paris.

centage growth rate. In addition the accuracy of national income statistics has been questioned. Computational errors and omissions in national income data cannot be denied, and neither can inconsistencies over time. Inaccuracy, it is suggested, is compounded where international comparisons of growth rates are made, since countries differ in the method of estimating national product. The authors of this study are not so pessimistic as to the reliability of data. The two countries studied here have well-developed national accounting procedures and the data utilized have been compiled for each country from OECD sources, and have therefore been subject to an element of standardization.[2]

A straightforward comparison of respective growth rates in the UK and West Germany is revealed in Figure 5.1, with the growth rate gap depicted in Figure 5.2. As is to be expected the growth rate is not constant over

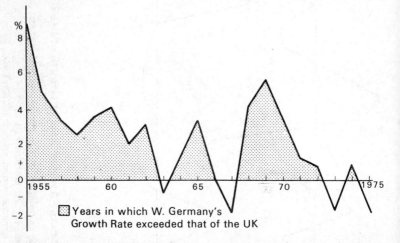

Figure 5.2 The Movement of the UK-West German Growth Rate Gap 1955-75

The vertical axis measures the difference in percentage growth rates of R.G.N.P.

time, it varies from year to year, although in both countries growth in this period has always been positive except in recent years. The growth rate is consistently higher in West Germany than in the United Kingdom – except in 1963, 1967, 1973 and 1975. The average annual rate of growth over the period was 2·8 per cent for the UK and 4·9 per cent for West Germany.

The evidence points to the conclusion that the United Kingdom growth performance has been poor relative to that of the West German economy. There may, however, be certain qualifications which need to be made when using a simple comparison of percentage growth rates of this kind. One must realize, for example, that the same percentage growth rate in each country may reflect differences in the absolute growth in output. If, for example, the real gross national product of country A is initially twice the absolute level of real gross national product in country B, then country B will have to grow at twice the percentage rate to maintain the absolute difference in real gross national product between the two countries.[3] Country A may not have fared as disastrously in absolute terms, as it has in percentage terms. In the case of the UK and West Germany, beginning in 1955, this particular kind of reassessment does not place the UK performance in any more favourable a light. By 1955 the absolute level of real national product in West Germany was already in excess of that of the UK, hence the UK would have needed to grow at a greater percentage rate per annum to catch up with the level of output in West Germany. Secondly, some economists[4] have argued that the international comparison which should be made is not that between actual growth rates in each country but one which compares each country's achievement of its growth potential, or capacity for growth.[5] For this reason there has been a considerable amount of empirical work directed towards assessing the UK's growth potential relative to those of other countries, including West Germany.[6] Adopting this approach, if it can be shown that the actual growth rate of the UK is nearer to its growth potential than the actual growth rate of West Germany is to its potential, one might conclude that the UK growth performance is better than that of West Germany. In what follows the reader should be able to recognize several forces acting upon growth in each country which do suggest that the growth potential in West Germany exceeds that of the UK.

WHY GROWTH RATES DIFFER – AN OVERVIEW

The aggregate output of any economy depends upon the input of labour to the production process and the average productivity of that labour, that is the average number of units of output yielded by each unit of labour employed.[7] The rate of growth of output must therefore depend upon the rate of growth of employed labour and the rate of growth of the productivity of the labour input.

Empirical evidence already undertaken concludes that the growth differential between the UK and West Germany is not to be explained by differential growth rates in labour input. Denison[8] found that, for the period 1950–62, none of the four major factors[9] influencing labour input contributed significantly towards higher average growth rates in West Germany. The average number of hours worked by the labour force declined more in West Germany than in the UK, thus making a negative contribution to the growth differential between the two countries. This was offset by a greater increase in the number of employed workers in West Germany compared with the UK, not attributable to a past higher population growth in West Germany, but partly to a utilization of unemployed labour, particularly in the period 1950–5. One must remember that in 1950 the UK was enjoying a relatively low unemployment rate of 1·3 per cent, compared with a level of 7·3 per cent of the labour force unemployed in West Germany. There was therefore much more unused productive potential in West Germany at that time than in the UK. However unemployment statistics for the later period 1955–75 would indicate that after 1955 West Germany no longer had the added bonus given to growth rates by a reduction in unemployment compared with the UK. Throughout the 1960s West Germany maintained an unemployment rate of less than 2 per cent, whereas the UK had an unemployment rate in excess of 2 per cent for the majority of years in that decade. Similarly there is no reason to suppose that differential changes in the standard of education between the two countries, or changes in the age and sex distribution of employed workers, had any more bearing upon growth differentials between 1955 and 1975, than Denison found them to have for the period 1950–62.

Differential growth therefore is to be explained by inequalities in the growth of labour productivity over the period 1955–75. The overall growth of labour productivity will to some extent depend upon the degree to which labour is transferred from sectors of low labour productivity to sectors of relatively high labour productivity. In virtually every country this reallocation would involve a switch of labour from agricultural to manufacturing employment. Knapp and Lomax[10] have emphasized that the growth potential of the UK was relatively low in the 1950s because of its inability to make a growth-beneficial reallocation of resources of this nature. The UK loses out for two reasons; not only is the proportion of labour employed in the agricultural sector lower in the UK than in most other countries and thus the possibility of transfers of labour lower, but the labour productivity gap between agricultural and manufacturing employment is lower, and therefore any transfers that do take place have a lower impact upon growth rates. Even an advanced economy, such as that of West Germany, had 11·4 per cent of its labour force employed in agriculture in 1965 compared with only 3·4 per cent in the UK, and thus the possibility of labour reallocation has been greater in West Germany than in the UK. Maddison has estimated the impact of such reallocation on productivity growth for the period 1950–60, finding that, on average, it yielded an additional 0·8 per cent per annum in West Germany against only 0·1 per cent per annum in the UK. The average gap in productivity growth between the two countries was 3·2 per cent per annum in this period, hence the elimination of this so-called disguised unemployment was far from a total explanation of growth difference. There is no evidence to suggest that the growth rate gap in the post-1960 period is to be explained to any greater degree by labour reallocation between agriculture and manufacturing. However one aspect of labour mobility which will be explored later in this chapter is the degree of movement of labour in both countries between manufacturing and tertiary sectors, and the impact it has upon growth.

Keynesian economists have stressed the role of investment in the growth process.[11] Expenditure on capital goods – that is expenditure on machinery, plant and equipment in particular – not only raises the productive potential of an economy, but also generates additional spending through the multiplier process. Balanced growth is achieved where the additional supply generated by investment is equal to the additional demand. If more capital equipment is combined with a given labour input one would expect the productivity of that labour to increase until the labour input becomes saturated with capital. For example, the farmer is more productive with a spade than without it; he is not necessarily more productive with two or more spades since he can only employ one spade at any one time. He would be more productive if, in place of the spade, he was given a tractor and a plough. This simple example demonstrates two things. The productivity of labour is changed by combining additional units of capital with labour. Secondly, through advances in knowledge and changes in the rate of application of that knowledge to the production process, that is through what the economist calls technological progress, the productivity of labour can be increased by changing the nature of the capital with which the labour input is combined. One question which this study seeks to answer is whether differential industrial fluctuation between West Germany and the UK has led to any significant differences in the amount of investment undertaken in each country, and the productivity of that investment.

Stress has been laid so far on changes in the input of labour and capital upon the rate of change of output. This suggests that growth is supply-led. As was hinted at above, growth will not automatically take place simply because more factor inputs become available for employment. The productive units in the economy, the firms, need an incentive to employ more factor inputs. This incentive is created by an increased desire on the part of consumers to buy commodities. Thus there is the prospect of demand-led growth. Growth is a complex process involving the interaction of supply and demand. Increases in supply are generated by increases in demand, or increases in demand are induced by increases in supply. Kindleberger[12] has emphasized that growth can be largely dependent upon the growth of demand in export markets – that is, growth is export-led. Again this is an issue which will enter into the following study, but let us begin by examining the nature of industrial fluctuation in the UK and West Germany in the last two decades.

INDUSTRIAL FLUCTUATIONS

The impact of fluctuation on economic performance and growth has been a recurring topic of discussion. Much literature has been concerned with the impact of the government's stabilization policies on the UK economy and on the so-called 'stop-go' pattern of post-war development.[13] Figure 5.1(b) illustrates the cyclical movement of the rate of economic growth of the UK economy. Periods of above average rates of growth have been associated with the tendency to move into over-full employment and inflationary conditions with a movement into external imbalance as the competitiveness of British goods deteriorated and the level of imports increased. By contrast the 'stop' periods have been accompanied by rising unemployment, as the price paid for the temporary improvement of the external situation. Table 5.1 illustrates the problem of apparently conflicting policy aims.

Table 5.1: The Movement of UK Policy Targets in Years of Peak Growth

Peak Years	Current Balance (£m)	Rate of Inflation
1960	−265	+3·4%
1964	−381	+4·7%
1968	−272	+5·5%
1973	−736	+10·1%

Whether the fluctuating pattern is the result of unavoidable policy conflicts, or of the deliberate or accidental mistiming, or directing, of macroeconomic policies by successive governments, is the subject of much debate.[14] The more pressing concern however is to examine whether short-term fluctuation is an important factor in accounting for the UK's declining and comparatively slow rate of economic growth. Alternatively we may prefer to suggest that fluctuations have been more harmful to the British economy than to other economies, in this case that of W. Germany, since it must be emphasized that all industrial countries in the post-war period have followed irregular and to a great extent similar paths of development. The increasing openness and interdependence of national economies have resulted in the more rapid international transmission of fluctuations and in the increased synchronization of fluctuations. Despite the commonality of experience, not all countries have found the fluctuations as costly as the UK, costly that is in terms of divergence from short-run policy targets and from long-run growth targets. Table 5.2 below provides information on the movement of West Germany's current balance and rate of inflation in boom years, which contrasts considerably with the UK experience depicted in Table 5.1.

Table 5.2 The Movement of West Germany's Policy Targets in Years of Peak Growth

Peak Growth Years	Current Balance (billion D.M.)	Rate of Inflation
1960	+4·68	+2·4%
1964	+0·15	+3·4%
1968	+10·67	+2·7%
1973	+2·47	+6·8%

The rate of inflation was consistently lower in West Germany than in the UK, and West Germany also avoided moving into current deficit in the years of maximum growth. The danger is that these short-term policy problems may be a consequence of the slower rate of economic growth in the UK, rather than a possible contributory factor in explaining the UK growth rate gap.

FLUCTUATIONS IN WHAT?

Fluctuations in economic activity may be identified in a variety of economic variables at both the aggregated and disaggregated levels over different periods of time. We could for instance seek to examine elements of instability in demand, output, employment and prices at the industry, sector, regional and national levels – on a monthly, quarterly and yearly basis. It may be the case that the macro picture or characteristics of economic flux or change will provide an insight into the UK's growth problems. Given therefore the post-war phenomenon of almost continuous growth of output and living standards the starting point for much research is to identify and measure fluctuations in annual rates of economic growth.

Figure 5.1 identifies fluctuations as deviations from the average annual rate of growth over the period, which was 2·8 per cent for the UK and 4·9 per cent for West Germany. While the average or trend rate of growth of the economy over a number of years is a somewhat arbitrary choice for the stable or target path of the economy, the diagram suggests that the absolute extent or degree of fluctuation has certainly not been greater in the UK than in West Germany in the post-war period. In fact a simple statistical measure of variation would indicate greater variation in the West German growth rates,[15] although a problem of comparison arises out of the possibility that a given amount of fluctuation is more costly or significant to a more slowly growing economy. This is an irreconcilable problem of weighting which complicates inter-country comparison, since, although it seems reasonable to argue that a fall in the annual growth rate of say 2 per cent below the trend will be more costly, and therefore of more consequence, to a country growing at 3 per cent on average than to one growing at 5 per cent, there is no clear criterion for weighting this common level of absolute fluctuation.

There is a general agreement amongst economists that, on the basis of a comparison of the amplitude of the fluctuation of GNP growth rates and industrial production, there appears no simple link between cyclical fluctuations and the trend rate of growth. Of course, there is more to fluctuation than the amount of deviation from the average. The number or frequency of up and downturns in the rate of economic activity may have significant repercussions. Alternatively the structure of the cycle, the breakdown into the length of time in which the economy is in relative boom as opposed to recession, may be a further significant variable. Is it the case that fluctuations have been more frequent, or that upturns have been shorter and downturns longer in duration in the UK than in West Germany? Figure 5.1 suggests that the frequency of fluctuations is fairly similar between the two countries, but that the UK has experienced a greater number of years of below-average growth. The annual data depicted however may be too crude to identify these dimensions of fluctuation satisfactorily. There may, for example, be a differential amount of quarterly fluctuation which is hidden by the annual data. In any case the distribution of time between boom and recession is sensitive to the choice of the trend. The mechanical exercise of calculating the average growth rate does not necessarily suitably separate boom and recession conditions. Table 5.3 below summarizes some of the conclusions of A. Whiting about the relative structure of UK and West German cycles.

Table 5.3 The Frequency and Structure of Post-War Fluctuations

| | *Average duration in quarters of :* | | |
	The full cycle	*Recession*	*Boom*
UK	17·2	7·7	9·5
W. Germany	16·8	8·0	8·8

Source: A. Whiting, 'An international comparison of the instability of economic growth', *Three Banks Review*, March 1976, p. 40.

The structure of fluctuations in the UK and West Germany appears remarkably similar (the UK in fact experienced slightly longer cycles and upturns). The conclusion therefore must be that the amplitude, frequency and time structure of the UK business cycle does not compare unfavourably with that of West Germany.

EXPANDING THE FRAMEWORK OF ANALYSIS

To dismiss the impact of fluctuation on the trend due to the similarity of the UK and West Germany aggregate picture, may overlook several possibilities:

1. the greater vulnerability of the UK economy to a given amount of fluctuation;
2. a very different pattern of fluctuation when each economy is disaggregated or when the relationships between demand and output are compared;
3. differential responses of the authorities to fluctuating conditions in the two countries.

One possibility would be to examine the breakdown of the instability of output on a sector or industry basis. It may be the case, for example, that the comparatively stable growth of total production in the UK hides evidence of very high instability in the potentially fast-growing industries. Such very high fluctuation could be offset by low instability areas of production, or could be self-cancelling if the individual industry cycles were out of phase with each other. This picture of industrial activity is, however, unlikely to be unique to the UK. There seems in fact no obvious reason to believe that the UK should have been unfortunate enough to possess a disproportionate amount of potentially fast-growing industries which have experienced high levels of fluctuation.

Rather than seek to disaggregate the supply or output side, we may seek to explain the greater vulnerability of the UK economy to an apparently similar degree of fluctuation by reference to differences in the changes in the pattern of demand over time; in particular we can refer to contrasts in the movement of aggregate spending (including foreign demand for domestic production) or domestic absorption[16] in relation to total or industrial production. Figure 5.3(a) and (b) compare the rates of growth of output and domestic absorption for the UK and West Germany. Examination of these identifies two potentially significant differences in the pattern of demand and output growth in the two countries. On the one hand there is a marked tendency for the growth of domestic spending to overshoot the growth of RGNP in the years of peak growth in the UK which is not evident in the case of West Germany. (Compare for example the years 1960, 1964, 1967 and 1972 in the two diagrams.) On the other, in every year the rate of growth of domestic absorption was positive in the UK, whereas for West Germany in the two problem years of 1967 and 1974 the level of absorption actually fell in absolute terms.

The picture of domestic- (in particular consumer-) led booms which

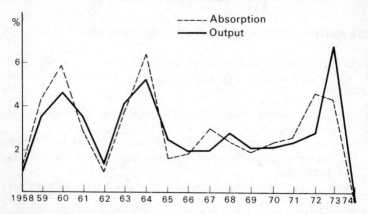

(a) The Growth of Output and Absorption in the UK. 1958-74.

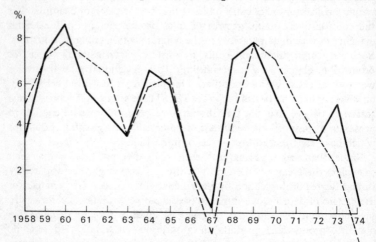

(b) The Growth of Output and Absorption in W. Germany, 1958-74.

Figure 5.3

tended to overshoot the growth of capacity is commonly echoed in the literature on the UK economy. Sensitivity to the problems of inflationary and external pressures has been heightened by the special position of sterling as an international reserve currency and by the threat of the loss of foreign currency reserves consequent upon the liquidation of foreign-held sterling balances. Nevertheless such recurrent conflict between growth and the balance of payments may have had important conse-quences for two potentially important sources of economic growth –

investment and exports. Table 5.4 below compares the share of RGNP devoted on average to spending on investment and exports in these two countries.

Table 5.4 Investment and Exports – Average Share of RGNP (%)

Years	UK Investment	Exports	W. Germany Investment	Exports
	%	%	%	%
1956–60	17	22	23	20
1961–65	19	22	26	20
1966–70	21	24	25	25
1971–75	17	24	25	33

INVESTMENT, EXPORTS AND FLUCTUATIONS

Despite the improvement in the proportion of RGNP devoted to both investment and exports up to 1970 in the UK, there has been a decline in the investment ratio during the 1970s. On the other hand the proportion devoted to investment has been consistently higher in W. Germany, while the export – RGNP ratio has increased significantly in the last decade. There is of course a danger of mistaking an effect of slower growth for an explanation of it, but nonetheless there is some evidence to suggest that exports and investment may be important factors in accounting for inter-country differences in rates of economic growth.

It is not the case that all countries have based their expansion on foreign markets (France is an example of a country with strongly based domestic expansion). West Germany is one of several economies however that give support to the export-led growth thesis. Similarly a high investment ratio (the ratio of investment to RGNP) does not guarantee rapid growth. On the one hand a high investment ratio does not ensure that the capital expenditure is of a nature or quality, or that it is directed into those areas, which will yield high output returns. On the other, a high level of capital accumulation does not ensure that the capital stock is fully or efficiently utilized. Hence not all countries with high investment ratios have high growth rates. Countries with low investment ratios however have tended not to grow quickly, and, if not a sufficient condition, a high investment ratio appears to be a necessary condition for raising growth potential. There would appear as such few dissenters from the argument that any attempt to raise the UK's growth potential will require an increase in the level of investment. The provision of more, and presumably more modern and efficient capital for the labour force, is necessary for the sustained growth of labour productivity. That increased provision may be facilitated by a reduction in the fluctuation and policy conflict which was identified in Figure 5.3(a).

It is not that reducing fluctuations will raise the trend growth rate because it will raise business confidence, reduce investment risks, or raise returns of capital by reducing the length of time that capital is under-utilized, and therefore increase the incentive to invest. Certainly investment may benefit as a result of such changes, but it has been shown that variations in output and capacity utilization have not been restricted to the UK. Fluctuations and high investment ratios are not incompatible, and we must therefore re-examine our conclusions about the differing pattern of output and demand growth in the UK and West Germany to see if that provides an explanation of these investment and export deficiencies; in particular we must consider how the pattern of the authorities' contrasting policy responses to these differing patterns of fluctuation may have contributed to these deficiencies.

THE IMPACT OF THE POLICY CYCLE

The greater tendency towards relatively over buoyant domestic conditions in the UK (namely the overshooting of demand in the upturn and the reluctance to push deflationary policies below the minimum required to stabilize the external situation) may well be explained by successive governments' unwillingness to allow the full burden of fluctuation to fall upon domestic employment. It may also help to explain the additional burden of fluctuation on the UK economy. Fluctuations and the cycle of policy may in fact have influenced exports and investment performance in the UK in the following ways:

1. Upturns and the associated rise in the demand for labour may have tended in the case of the UK to cause a more rapid rise in wages and earnings due to a low rate of labour mobility into the rapidly growing sectors. That immobility may be accounted for by the impact of trade unions and government on the labour market; the result was a growth of wages and costs in excess of productivity which was not reversed in the downturn due to the downward rigidity of wages and costs. Thus the uneven growth of demand and productivity has tended to give an extra push to the prices spiral and UK loss of competitiveness. Figure 5.4 demonstrates the impact of declining competitiveness of exports on the growth of exports in 1967 and 1972 in the UK. The lagged impact of this slowing down of export growth was identified for the years 1968 and 1973 in Table 5.1.

2. The immobility of labour in the UK may be related to the role of the UK authorities in the labour market, and their attempts to minimize the impact of cyclical variations upon employment. During periods of rising unemployment in the private manufacturing sector in particular, the authorities have tended to absorb labour into the

public sector in order to stabilize the overall employment situation. With the revival of manufacturing activity labour shortages especially of skilled labour have soon become evident, because either the labour absorbed into the public sector became permanently employed or because these labour market conditions discouraged the retraining of labour.

The effects of this policy-response pattern to industrial fluctuations has been two-fold. On the one hand the growth of the public sector (especially in the area of the provision of usually non-marketed goods, e.g. social services, education and public administration) and therefore of government spending, and the buoyancy of consumer spending has meant that a diminishing proportion of national output has been available for either investment in the private sector (in private manufacturing in particular) or for the balance of trade (exports minus imports). Figure 5.4 for instance illustrates the marked tendency for the growth of exports to be at the expense of the growth of private investment in the UK, especially in the years 1964, 1967 and 1969. Except in the problem year of 1967, in West Germany a conflict between private investment and exports is less evident.

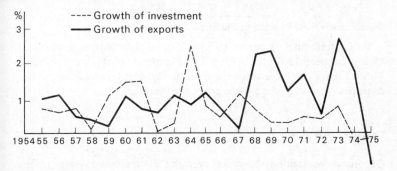

Figure 5.4 The Contributions (1) of Investment and Exports to the Growth of RGNP in the UK, 1955-75

(1) Changes in investment and exports were expressed against the level of RGNP in the previous year—

$$\frac{\triangle I}{Y_{t-1}} \text{ and } \frac{\triangle X}{Y_{t-1}}$$

The growth of the UK public sector on the other hand and the slow growth of investment in private manufacturing industry (Figure 5.4 shows that gross private investment has grown very slowly since 1965) has brought about important structural changes in the UK economy. The decline in the manufacturing sector's growth potential brought about by the relative shift of labour away from manufacturing activities is emphasized by Table 5.5, and contrasts markedly with the stability of manufacturing employment in W. Germany. The significance of the 8·6 per cent fall in the manufacturing sector's share of employment between 1962–73 for the growth of manufacturing output and therefore UK growth is exaggerated by the slow growth of investment already identified.

Table 5.5: The Percentage of the Labour Force Employed in Manufacturing

Year	UK	W. Germany
1962	34·3	38·9
1963	33·4	38·7
1964	33·4	38·8
1965	33·0	39·3
1966	32·5	39·3
1967	31·4	38·7
1968	31·0	39·0
1969	31·0	40·0
1970	30·6	40·5
1971	27·6	40·2
1972	26·3	39·7
1973	25·7	39·8

Source: *Labour Force Statistics*, various years, O.E.C.D, Paris.

By contrast manufacturing industry's share of employment increased slightly between 1962 and 1973 in West Germany and this was associated with a higher rate of investment growth. The consequences for the two countries' growth potential are fairly predictable.

CONCLUSIONS

One must be cautious however over the interpretation given to the relationship between growth potential, fluctuations, and the cycle of economic policy. Certainly the UK has experienced a slower rate of economic growth on average than West Germany, and a decline in growth potential associated with the decline in the size of its manufacturing sector by employment share in the last two decades. Similarly the UK has been subject to a different pattern of fluctuation and policy response – the so-called 'stop-go' pattern of development. Whether slower economic growth is a cause or consequence of fluctuation and of the conflict between investment and export growth is open to debate. The initial sections of the case in fact illustrate the complexities of the growth process, of the inter-relationships between aggregate demand and supply, and the problems of answering the question why growth rates differ. This case has emphasized one aspect of any comparison of national growth rates; namely the impact of fluctuations in aggregate domestic spending on industrial structure and growth potential.

REFERENCES

1. *See* O. Morgenstern, *On the Accuracy of Economic Observations*, Princeton Univ. Press, 1963, p. 287.
2. The main source is the National Accounts of the OECD countries.
3. A simple numerical example will demonstrate this point:

	RNP (Yr1)	% Growth	RNP (Yr2)
Country A	100	5%	105
Country B	50	10%	55

Even though Country B has grown at twice the percentage rate as Country A, the absolute difference between their RNPs has remained the same (50).
4. *See*, for example, 'The British Growth Performance', J. Knapp and K. Lomax. *Lloyds Bank Review*, October 1964.
5. Again a numerical example will illustrate this:

	Actual Growth (%)	Potential Growth (%)
Country A	1·5	2·0
Country B	3·0	6·0

Although a straightforward comparison would suggest B's performance is 'better' than that of A, by taking account of growth potentials one could argue that A has achieved 75 per cent of its growth potential whereas B has only achieved 50 per cent of its potential. Therefore A's performance is 'better' than that of B.
6. In particular the work undertaken at the National Institute for Economic Research.
7. $Q = L \frac{(Q)}{(L)}$

Q = aggregate output
L = labour input
Q/L = average product of labour.
8. E. Denison, *Why Growth Rates Differ*, Brookings Institute, Washington, 1967.
9. These were: (a) hours worked
   (b) number of employed persons
   (c) age and sex distribution of employed workers
   (d) education of employed workers.
10. Knapp and Lomax, *op. cit.*
11. This emphasis is to be found in the Harrod-Domar Growth Model.

12. C. Kindleberger, *Internatioenal Economics*, 5th Ed, Irwin, 1973.
13. *See*, for example, P. D. Henderson (ed.), *Economic Growth in Britain*, Weidenfeld & Nicolson, 1966.
14. *See* A. R. Prest (ed.), *A Manual of Applied Economics*, Weidenfeld & Nicolson, 1966.
15. E. Lundberg, *Instability and Economic Growth*, Yale, U.P. 1967, reaches a similar conclusion on the basis of a consideration of a range of measures of instability.
16. Domestic absorption is the sum of consumer, investment and government spending. Changes in absorption were expressed in relation to GNP. (Y) in the previous year (i.e. the change in absorption divided by Y) in order to make them directly comparable with the rate of growth of GNP.

QUESTIONS FOR DISCUSSION

1. The high inflation of recent years has led to rapid increases in the value of output. Why is this increase not an indication of high growth rates?

2. Why might a positive growth rate of RGNP not signify an increase in the standard of living?

3. Why is the growth potential of an economy which has had a late start in the industrialization process expected to be higher than an old industrialized economy?

4. What are the possible causes of an increase in the average productivity of labour in an economy discussed in the text?

5. What forces within the EEC are responsible for the increasing synchronization of cyclical fluctuations among member states?

6. In what ways may government stabilization policies themselves generate or increase industrial fluctuations? Illustrate your answer with reference to the post-war experience of the UK.

7. To what extent is variation around the average, annual rate of economic growth of an economy an ideal measure of economic fluctuation?

8. Why may fluctuations have heightened the competition between investment and exports for industrial output in the UK? Provide contrasting examples from the West German economy.

9. How important do you think investment is to raising the rate of economic growth?

10. For what reasons may the attempts to minimize the impact of fluctuations on employment have hampered economic growth in the UK?

Teacher's Notes

The United Kingdom's Public Sector Debt

TEACHER'S NOTES

In general terms the case study endeavours to emphasize the way in which the public sector debt position has changed since about 1973 and teachers will probably want to stress that these changes have been due to the abnormal economic circumstances prevailing in the years in question. The present government may be seen as being in a difficult dilemma: it could reduce the borrowing requirement and the rate of inflation but only at the risk of a drastic increase in unemployment. In a televised interview in December 1976 Mr Healey estimated that a balanced budget for the financial year 1975/6 would have entailed unemployment rising to over 3 million.

There is room for considerable emphasis on the inadequacy of the official statistics available. The Radcliffe Report commented:

> Although the National Debt, in the sense in which we are using the term, is of such great interest for economic policy, there is in existing publications no adequate statistical analysis of it, nor indeed is there any statement of its size, either in published documents or in any official papers that have been brought to our notice. The great advance in official statistical knowledge of national income has not been matched by any comparable advance in knowledge of national assets and liabilities.[1]

The position has, of course, improved considerably since 1959. It is interesting to speculate, for example, on the accuracy of the figure quoted later in the study for depreciation of the government's property and capital assets and to consider how one might arrive at a figure for depreciation on a school, hospital, motorway, or power-station.

The 'public sector borrowing requirement' (PSBR) is a formulation that has been much in the news: it is defined as:

> the extent to which the public sector borrows from other sectors of the economy and overseas to finance the balance of expenditure and receipts arising from its various activities,

i.e. it is the *annual* figure corresponding to the total in Table 1.2, *less* the double-counting referred to in the text. The Treasury publication *Economic Progress Report*, No. 69, issued in December 1975, showed clearly the distinctions between 'PSBR', 'current deficit' and 'financial deficit'.

Radcliffe Report

The quotations from the Radcliffe Report have been deliberately kept brief in the text of the case study but in fact the first quotation continued:

> If the achievement of this result threatens to entail growth of cash or other highly liquid liabilities to a degree thought dangerous, because of the repercussions of this growth of liquidity in the private sector, the authorities have in theory three courses open to them:
>
> 1. they can make long-term securities so much more attractive than the threat is averted (i.e. 'funding' succeeds);
> 2. they can increase taxation, so enabling themselves to get the real resources they want without adding so much to, and perhaps even bringing about some reduction of the National Debt;
> 3. they can cut the use of real resources by the public sector (cutting either current Government expenditure or investment in the public sector) so reducing the amount of debt to be placed with the private sector in the period.[2]

The Report stated that there had been in the 1950s examples of all three methods of adjustment. At the present time of course there is much attention on the third possible course of action. The Report's assessment of the problems involved in each of these courses remains still very relevant. It said:

> The second method solves the problem by the compulsion of the tax system, which theoretically enables the public sector to hold the real resources it requires without embarking on the kind of debt operations it is striving to avoid. It cannot be resorted to without serious thought of the strains upon the taxation system and intricate repercussions on the disposition of people to spend or save; but these complexities have to be faced whenever taxation has to be increased. Its traditional appeal as 'sound finance' is based on the common prudence of paying one's way, but this is an argument that loses much of its force when the Budget deficit is being used in effect to finance additions to the productive equipment of the economy.[3]

The Chancellor, Dennis Healey, has publicly indicated his wish to lower the tax burden of higher income earners in 1977. Thus higher personal taxation at the present time is regarded as being highly unacceptable. Of its third specified course for debt management, the Radcliffe committee said:

> The third method – adaptation by cutting the use of resources in the public sector – may be facilitated by a change of circumstances, as when an easing of international tension permits a reduction in defence expenditure. Without such good fortune it means that the exigencies of debt policy force society to spend less than it intended on public needs. This is a confession of failure;

it may entail wasteful disruption of plans, as when investment in the public sector was cut for this kind of reason in 1957.[4]

The Radcliffe assessment of the first option is very relevant to the recent discussion of the government 'crowding out' funds for private industry. Its view was:

> The first method – making attractive the holding of the debt with an acceptable composition – has obvious attractions, in that it allows society to proceed with its plans for the public sector without undesirable disturbance of the fiscal system. The debt manager's aim must be to strive for solution by this method, and it is essentially a matter of finding an interest rate structure that will ensure the desired structure of the debt. Yet it is not a method that leaves the distribution of resources untouched: as we have seen in Chapter VI, even if higher interest rates do not promote increased saving (as they perhaps do), they certainly discourage, though slowly and in limited areas, investment in the private sector. A higher rate of interest designed to attract firm holders of Government securities thus operates not only as a protection for the real needs of the public sector but also acts over a period as a force gradually releasing resources from the private sector. It must not be supposed that this implies a conflict between debt policy and employment policy: it is rather that, in managing the debt, the authorities must resist the temptation to push interest rates so high in order to get the debt firmly held, that they engender a slow but damaging decline in activity.[5]

The Report still thus offers a very useful perspective on the more recent problems of economic policy.

There is room for considerable class discussion here about the interaction between the debt and macroeconomic policy. The various attempts to curtail the growth in public expenditure commencing with the mini-budget of December 1973 should be appreciated after looking at recent *Economic Progress Reports*. With regard to possible increases in taxation, students will obviously realize that these are usually unpopular in political terms and would be avoided by any Chancellor if at all possible: at the same time however, they should be familiar with the 'buoyancy' of the UK tax system due to the progressiveness of our largest single tax, the income tax. The effect of this is that during any period of rising prices the government's revenue, in real terms, automatically tends to increase.

The link with the Money Supply is most easily seen via the issue of Treasury Bills which *expand* the banks' credit base (in the official view, at least) but reference should also be made to the issue of long-term stock which is paid for by remittances from bank accounts, thus *decreasing* the Money Supply. To a very limited extent some extra debt may be financed by the issue of further currency but the extreme circumstances experienced under the Weimar Republic show clearly what can happen if such a policy is pushed too far.

The 'burden' arguments in the last section may be too complex and abstract for many students although this topic provides a good example of the way in which eminent economists can continue a disagreement over a period of many years. The students might be invited to consider whether similar disagreements are to be found in the other subjects they study.

REFERENCES

1. *Report*, para. 536, pp. 191–2.
2. *Ibid.*, para. 558, p. 207.
3. *Ibid.*, para. 559, p. 207.
4. *Ibid.*, para. 560, p. 207.
5. *Ibid.*, para. 561, pp. 207–8

FURTHER READING

The *Bank of England Quarterly Bulletin* contains an article annually on the latest position of the National Debt, including its structure and composition. An introduction to the general subject of the debt is to be found in both A. R. Prest: *Public Finance*, Weidenfeld & Nicolson, and G. C. Hockley: *Monetary Policy and Public Finance*, Routledge & Kegan Paul. *See also* 'The National Debt', *Economic Progress Report*, No. 44, April 1974, pp. 2–4.

The links with monetary policy are made clear in S. Brittan: *Steering the Economy*, Pelican 1971, in many articles in the *Midland Bank Review*, and in more specialized articles in the other bank reviews: these are too numerous to mention in detail. There are good chapters on monetary policy in J. C. R. Dow, *The Management of the British Economy 1945–60*, CUP. 1964, R. Caves (ed.), *Britain's Economic Prospects* Allen & Unwin, 1968, and C. D. Cohen, *British Economic Policy 1960–69* Butterworths, 1971. For reading on the 'burden' arguments, *see* under 'References'.

POINTS INTENDED TO BE RAISED FROM THE QUESTIONS

1. In a climate of reducing public expenditure, the provision of more detailed statistics seems unlikely but in the absence of them our knowledge of some aspects of the debt is necessarily incomplete. Here it is worth examining the footnotes to Table 1.6 and considering, for example, the effects of switching the basis of assessment of stocks from market values to book values.
2. Little further comment is needed here except to emphasize the wholesale acceptance of Keynesian policy since 1945. The aims of

policy mentioned in the text may conflict with each other. Most commentators agree that the stated aim of the Chancellor was usually a reduction in unemployment although for much of the period the balance-of-payments situation was in fact the effective constraint. Post-1973 the rates of inflation previously unknown in this country caused attitudes to change.

3. With regard to the debt itself the position is extremely worrying: borrowing to cover *current* running expenditure cannot easily be defended. However, this point cannot be seen in isolation from the quite exceptional economic circumstances of the years in question. Students might be invited to consider the Chancellor's dilemma and discuss what they would do in his position. The political position of the government, with a very small majority in the House of Commons, should also be mentioned.

4. One must recognize the validity of the Bank of England's fears re financing the debt with both additional debt, and maturing stock to be replaced, each year, but until 1971 their caution was perhaps exaggerated. The financial institutions have large additional sums to invest each year and necessarily must place part in gilt-edged stock: it is unlikely that they would be dissuaded by relatively minor fluctuations in the market. Since 1971 (*Competition and Credit Control*), the market seems to work perfectly well on its own except in emergencies, although we have no way of knowing how much intervention by the Bank of England still takes place.

5. The answer seems to be Yes. Consider how independent use of open market operations and interest rate manipulations has often not been possible. C. D. Cohen, *op cit.*, provides interesting detail on this point.

6. A budget deficit will *increase* the Money Supply if financed by (i) the issue of extra currency (which must be limited) or (ii) Treasury Bills (following the view that these increase the banks' credit base), or *decrease* the Money Supply if the issue of gilt-edged stock deprives the purchasers of cash. Whatever the initial effect, it can if necessary be offset by the Bank of England via their day-to-day manipulations of stock. If the deficit was to reduce unemployment, a relatively small increase in the Money Supply might be not unwelcome. *See* 'Britain's money supply', Business Brief in *The Economist*, 27 November 1976, pp. 88–89.

7. Such decisions are in reality more political than economic but LAs and PCs cannot expect to be immune from factors affecting the remainder of the national economy.

8. The obvious effect is on the level of investment but it is also worth considering whether consumption would be affected (via, for instance, the cost of hire purchase transactions). Higher interest rates will also attract international liquid funds into the country with consequent

effects on the value of sterling and on liquidity generally. The 'circumstances' relate to the aims mentioned previously. If the servicing costs rise, extra tax revenue will be required to pay for these. *See* B. Reading, 'Too High interest rates', *National Westminster Bank Quarterly Review*, February 1970, and the comments on this article by N. Peera' 'Interest rates: illusion or reality' in the same journal in its May 1970 issue, pp. 40–47 and P. Wann, 'Lower interest rates?', *ibid.* pp. 48–54.

9. The Bank of England constantly manipulates stock, e.g. it will buy in quantities of any stock approaching its redemption date, and any new stock may be released to the market gradually over a period of months, rather than suddenly. Market fluctuations are thus minimized.

10. Not only was there no extra debt in those years but the surpluses meant that some maturing stock did not need to be replaced. Hence *Competition and Credit Control* could promise (i) a freely fluctuating gilt-edged market, (ii) more use of open market operations, (iii) an ending of directives, and (iv) more fluctuations in interest rates. The 1972 sterling crisis severely curtailed the operation of the new system. Subsequently the 'Supplementary Deposits Scheme' (to be distinguished from Special Deposits) represented a new attempt at control. *See* 'Banking in Slumpflation', Schools Brief in *The Economist*, 3 May 1976, pp. 32–3, reprinted in *What's Going On?*, The Economist, 1975, pp. 14–15, and J. Hough, 'Monetary policy', pp. 14–17 in P. Maunder (ed.), *Macroeconomics in Question*, Economics Association, 1975.

11. In summary, *re* (i) there is a relative burden but not an absolute one, (ii) the answer depends on whether we would otherwise have to divert savings from e.g. private sector investment. Debt financing for *current* expenditure must always constitute a burden. However, there is a danger in such simplified statements in view of the complexity of the topic. Mishan's essay, *op cit.*, is a very readable statement of the 'anti-burden' case.

CASE STUDY TWO
The Economics of Scottish Independence

TEACHER'S NOTES

The debate on the economics of Scottish independence has been in progress in Scotland for over ten years. There have been two main phases. Up to 1974 the debate was centred on the proposition that Scotland was able to enjoy the living standards it had because of the Union with England and Wales; Scotland was, in fact, *subsidized* by the United Kingdom as a whole. This subsidy took the form of an excess of expenditure over revenue on the government's account (McCrone, 1969) and an unknown, but suspected, deficit on the trading account. The conclusion drawn from these accounts (H. M. Treasury, 1969; McCrone, 1969; Alexander, 1970) was that independence would lead to a fall in living standards because the effective subsidy provided by the United Kingdom would be withdrawn. This was hotly contested by Scottish National Party in an alternative estimate of the Scottish budget (SNP, 1969). The budget prepared by economists in the SNP is shown in Table 2.5 (Johnston, 1971). The SNP's figures show Scotland with a surplus for 1967/68 of £30 million instead of a deficit of £476 million (Treasury) or £211 million (McCrone, 1969).

The major areas of disagreement between the estimates are in the matter of the extent to which Scottish citizens work in Scotland for UK firms with headquarters in England and in consequence are assessed for taxation purposes as if they were working in England. The SNP claimed that 29·5 per cent of Scots taxpayers were in this position and therefore the Scottish taxation contribution was understated. A similar situation exists, it was claimed, in respect of corporation taxation. By the very nature of these facts the amount collected in revenue must be indeterminate with a possible margin of error in either direction of some millions. Another contentious argument occurred over the amount of unallocated expenditure credited to Scotland. The McCrone estimates allocated £291 million to Scotland from defence, external relations, debt interest and other services while the SNP allocated a much lower figure of £247 million.

The debate was inconclusive. The nature of the data made it impossible to be certain whether the estimates corresponded to the real position. By varying the assumptions different results could be achieved. This still left another part of the argument out of the discussion. This related to whether an independent Scotland would pursue the economic policies experienced in Scotland since the war which, whatever their merits or otherwise, contributed in some measure to the relative size of the Scottish gross domestic product. If other policies had been pursued and as a result Scotland had operated at a lower level of spare capacity it might have been possible for Scotland to fund any deficit that existed out of domestic resources, assuming that the deficit was not large and that such policies were possible.

The second phase of the debate began sometime after the realization of the vast oil reserves available in the North Sea in the Scottish sector of the United Kingdom exploration and exploitation zone. It took some time for the debate to get going and it is continuing at present. The oil resources altered the deficit position immediately. Assuming some Scottish sovereignty over the oil revenues (itself a political issue) the revenue account to the government would swing into substantial surplus. This would also cover any trade deficit, net of property income from abroad, that Scotland was running in the 1960s (Begg, 1975). Inside the UK, Scotland was now clearly going to be 'subsidizing' England. There are a number of conceptual problems in the idea of 'subsidization' that will permit a debate to continue on this point. It could be argued that as the central government imposes the taxes on the oil flow it is the central government that should be considered as the receiver of the taxation and not the region of the United Kingdom that happens to generate the activity that is taxed. In much the same way, taxation on whisky consumption should be seen as a central government activity and not as a credit to the region that produces the Scotch. This kind of thinking has been applied by a recent report on Scottish Devolution (Henley, 1976) which debits Scotland with the foreign investment costs of North Sea oil exploration (running at about £1,200 million in 1975–6) and credits the UK with the future oil revenues that will arise as a result of the investment. Not surprisingly, the report concludes that Scottish independence would not be possible as it could not afford to raise the investment funds for the oil, and that as a result the per capita import deficit in Scotland is several times that for the UK as a whole, which means Scotland is running a trade deficit of about 20 per cent of the GNP.

The central issues in the oil balance are as follows:

1. How much of the oil in the North Sea would come under Scottish sovereignty?
2. For which foreign currencies will that share be sold?
3. How will Scotland dispose of this foreign exchange?
4. How much of the oil earnings will be consumed and how much invested in physical capital imports?
5. Will Scotland be able to raise man-hour productivity in domestic manufacturing (and secure enough economic growth to absorb

Table 2.5 The Scottish Budget: Treasury and SNP Estimates 1967/8

Current Account

Current Revenue	Treasury	SNP	Current Expenditure	Treasury	SNP
Income Tax	274	330	Identified Government Expenditure	674	780
Surtax	18	20	Grants to Local Authorities	170	} 780
Profits tax	3	3		844	780
Corporation Tax	85	115			
Less Transitional relief	−3	−6			
	377	462	*Allocated Expenditure*		
Taxes on Expenditure	341	393	Defence	222	152
Motor Vehicle Duty	21	23	External Relations	20	20
SET	30	30	Other Services	4	9
Stamp Duties	6	6	Debt Interest	111	66
ITA Levy	1			357	247
National Insurance	175	185			
Gross Trading Surplus	15	—			
Rent	2	—			
Interest on Loans	83	74			
Miscellaneous Receipts	10	22			
	684	724			
Total Current Revenue	1061	1186	Total Current Expenditure	1201	1027

Capital Account

Capital Receipts	Treasury	SNP	Capital Expenditure	Treasury	SNP
Taxes on Capital	37	37	Identified Capital Exp	141	} 175
			Grants to LA's	19	
			Grants to Public Corporations	2	
			UK Expenditures Allocated at 9·4%	16	—
			Loans to LAs, Public Authorities	195	—
			To Total Capital Payments	373	175
			Total Capital Expenditures	−336	−138

Total Deficit/Surplus on Current and Capital Accounts

Treasury 1061−1201−336 = −£476m SNP 1186−1027−138 = +£30m

Sources: (Treasury, 1969; SNP, 1969). Extracted from Johnston (1971) Tables 7.6, 7.7, pp. 172–3, 176–7.

surplus labour) fast enough to offset any rise in the Scottish exchange rate?

6. Can any surplus oil revenues be absorbed externally either in domestic acquisition of foreign holdings or in foreign acquisition of foreign holdings?

7. Can Scotland transform the industrial base with a view to the post-oil years after 2040?

In this context the Simpson Plan (Simpson, 1976) is a possible basis for discussion. Its economics may not survive its political practicality. However, it does outline one arrangement that could be negotiated between Scotland and England. The issue here is one of Scotland ensuring that England undertakes the real resource transfer necessary to re-equip Scottish industry; the Simpson Plan ensures that the transfer will take place because Scotland will be a sovereign and equal partner to the division of the oil resources. The alternative for Scotland on relying on centrally directed regional policies (the current 1976 position) or on the subordinate partnership of devolution (the 1978 position) does not ensure that the transfer will be effected; it remains subject ot the goodwill and political choices of the UK parliament.

It has been suggested (Tait, 1976) that devolution as proposed by the government, with the economic powers firmly retained at Westminster, will create a 'knife-edge' problem: centrally directed stabilization policies will effectively prevent locally initiated economic policies through the Scottish Assembly but will require politically unpopular transfers of resources from the more affluent regions, or, devolved Assemblies will tend to operate as separate countries. The 'in-between stages are unstable' (Tait, 1976, p. 10).

If the alternatives are centralization or separatism it follows that the issues discussed in this case study are going to be in dispute for much of the next ten years.

REFERENCES

K. J. W. Alexander (University of Strathclyde), 'The Economic Case Against Independence', in Neil MacCormick (University of Edinburgh) (ed.), *The Scottish Debate : Essays on Scottish Nationalism*, Oxford UP, London, 1970.

H. M. Begg, C. M. Lythe, R. Sorley (University of Dundee), *Expenditure in Scotland 1961–1971*, Scottish Academic Press, Edinburgh, 1975.

Henley Centre for Forecasting, *The Scottish Economy 1980, London, 1976.*

H. M. Treasury, *A Scottish Budget : Estimates of Central Government Revenue and Expenditure Attributable to Scotland for the Financial Year, 1967–8*, HMSO, London, October 1969.

T. J. Johnston, N. K. Buxton, D. Mair (Heriot-Watt University), *Structure and Growth of the Scottish Economy*, Collins, London, 1971.

Gavin McCrone (University of Glasgow – Scottish Office), *Scotland's Future: The Economics of Nationalism*, Blackwell, Oxford, 1969.

Scottish National Party, Research Department, *Who Says We Need Subsidies? The Treasury's Scottish Budget Analysed*, Scottish National Party, Edinburgh, November, 1969.

David Simpson (University of Strathclyde), 'Scotland, England and North Sea Oil', in Gavin Kennedy (University of Strathclyde) (ed.), *The Radical Approach: papers on an independent Scotland*, Palingenesis Press, Edinburgh, 1976.

Alan A. Tait (University of Strathclyde), *The Economics of Devolution: a Knife-Edge Problem*, Fraser of Allander Institute Speculative Paper No. 2, Scottish Academic Press, Edinburgh, 1975.

FURTHER READING

C. Blake, 'The Effectiveness of Investment Grants as a Regional Subsidy', *Scottish Journal of Political Economy*, Vol. xix, No. 1, February, 1972.

Gordon Brown (ed.), *The Red Paper on Scotland*, Edinburgh University Student Publications Board, Edinburgh, 1975.

Gordon Cameron, 'Economic Analysis of a Declining Urban Economy', *Scottish Journal of Political Economy*, Vol. 8, No. 3, 1973.

——and G. L. Reid, *Scottish Economic Planning and the Attraction of Industry*, Oliver and Boyd, Edinburgh, 1966.

Gavin Kennedy (ed.), *The Radical Approach: papers on an independent Scotland*, Palingenesis Press, Edinburgh, 1976.

Gavin McCrone, *Scotland's Economic Progress, 1951–1960*, Allen & Unwin, London, 1965.

—— *Regional Policy in Britain*, London, 1969.

D. I. McKay, 'Industrial Structure and Regional Growth: a methodological Problem', *Scottish Journal of Political Economy*, Vol. 15, No. 2, 1968.

—— (ed.) *Scotland 1980*, Q Press, Edinburgh, 1977.

R. Maurice (ed.), *National Accounts Statistics sources and methods*, Central Statistical Office, HMSO, London, 1968.

George T. Murray, *Scotland: The New Future*, STV, Blackie, Glasgow, 1973.

David Simpson, 'Independence: the economic issues' in Neil MacCormick (ed.), *The Scottish Debate: Essays on Scottish Nationalism*, Oxford UP., London, 1970.

John M. Stopford and Louis T. Wells, *Managing the Multi-National Enterprise: organization of the firm and ownership of subsidaries*, Longman, London, 1972.

POINTS INTENDED TO BE RAISED FROM THE QUESTIONS

1. An economic region that has been part of a much larger economy for a long time such as Scotland has since the Treaty of Union of 1707, is bound to be greatly influenced by the economic relationship. The economic situation will be a product both of the innate characteristics of the region (geography, climate, natural resources, culture of its peoples, including attitudes towards change, risk and incentives) and the characteristics and experiences of the larger region (system of government, economic record, rate of growth, distribution of industry between the regions, sector composition of economic activity, world trade position and so on). The description of this relationship involves a study of these characteristics.

   Separating these influences out in order to assign weights to their influence on the current situation is extremely difficult and prone to controversy. It follows that it is extremely difficult to be precise about what effects a real separation will have on the regional economy. In the real world we only experience the choices we actually make and it is nigh impossible to decide whether it would be better/worse to have chosen an alternative. This is true for the choice between independence or union, membership of the EEC or withdrawal, repeal or continuation of the Corn Laws, or free trade or protection.

2. The assumption is that exactly the same budgetary programme of a UK Government in Scotland would be followed by an independent Scottish government. This is not necessarily true. A change in the mix of expenditure is feasible as no particular mix is inevitable or ordained. It is possible to reduce certain expenditures without reducing the standard of living in a significant way, e.g., if some defence expenditure was cut that was not spent in Scotland anyway or fewer expensive embassies were maintained where Scottish interests were marginal or non-existent. Raising some taxes might reduce some people's living standards in order to maintain or increase other people's. If inter-personal comparisons are not feasible it is impossible to say whether this raises overall living standards or not.

   An alternative for the Scottish government might be to run the economy at a higher level of capacity utilization. The fall in unemployment and the increase in domestic output will increase the taxable capacity of the economy without necessarily reducing living standards. The problem is whether this is a feasible policy in view of the relationship with England and international effects on the Scottish economy.

3. Inter-regional trade flows and monetary movements are not recorded. This means that national product, which includes net property

income from abroad and other regions, cannot be known. Domestic product can be estimated because it does not involve trade and monetary movements. Domestic value added (McCrone's method, 1969) or Domestic Expenditure (Begg's method, 1975) can be estimated from available data.

For opponents of independence these kind of figures provide further evidence that Scotland would face a reduction in its living standards if it had to carry such deficits on the balance of trade. In the absence of data on the net property income from abroad it is not possible to say whether the actual balance of payments would be brought into surplus or even greater imbalance when the two figures were added together. A strong positive contribution from net property income (earnings by resident Scots from investments abroad exceeding earnings by foreigners from investments in Scotland) would reduce the crude trade balance and perhaps eliminate it.

4. The most important caveat is the relative crude nature of the method of estimating. Several disparate sources have to be used to arrive at a final figure (e.g., Inland Revenue statistics, Family Expenditure Survey, Department of Trade and Industry accounts, National Food Survey Expenditure accounts, Local Government Financial Statistics, among others). Another problem is in arriving at compatibility in the price series – current or constant prices. Residual errors when grossed up can produce wide margins of error.

The relevant method is to use the identities:

$$Y = C + I + G + (X - M) - (T - S)$$
and
$$E = C + I + G - (T - S)$$
therefore
$$Y - E = X - M$$

This puts the entire difference between product and expenditure on to the balance of trade in goods and services. If the errors are large the trade balance will be distorted.

The second most important caveat is the fact that this method excludes information about the real balance of payments because it excludes net property income from abroad. Also in a regional account the figures do not show the relative trade balances of the region with the rest of the world and the region with the parent economy. A region could be in substantial surplus with the rest of the world and in deficit with the parent economy; if the inter-regional relationship precludes adjustment within the region to eliminate a region–parent deficit it may be that the overall deficit is involuntary though avoidable.

In food output Scotland is well placed, compared to England, because of its substantially lower import dependence. Increased domestic production of food would reduce food imports even more and produce a surplus for export. A well-protected fishing industry would also provide considerable scope for exports. Industrial investment, either to modernize existing industry or to expand into new industries, is crucial to the creation of employment opportunities in the future. Scottish productivity in many sectors is lower than that of comparable sectors in the UK, which are themselves lower than in other countries. Economic policies to achieve these objectives are certainly feasible and they would have an impact on the trade balance by either import substitution or export expansion. Again this is an area where it is impossible to be specific about the actual course of events.

5. External control does have important effects on an economy. The balance between innovating, entrepreneurial type of decision-making and routinized managerial supervision worsens. Branch plants are receivers of allocated handouts of investment, sales, and products; they seldom have the research and development resources for independent product and market development. They are therefore vulnerable to markets they are restrained from competing freely in and to the efficiency, or competence, of higher managerial decisions taken by personnel outside of the country. Pricing and profit policy is decided by the central management and this can mean manipulative costing through transfer pricing and licence charges which make the branch factory a book 'loss-maker' or close to it. The economics of these operations may look worse than they are.

The policy response to the growth of multinational operations and the negative effects mentioned above can be taken by government. Companies can be required to set up R and D functions as a condition of operation, and certainly as a condition for receiving state subsidies and grants. They can be compelled to incorporate their company in the country with a majority role for nationals and residents. Legislation can be enacted to forbid transfer pricing and bogus licence charges. Profits taxes can be adjusted to give an incentive to companies that comply with such approved practices.

6. World oil prices are upwards of $11·50 a barrel. These prices are set by the Organisation of Petroleum Exporting Countries, which is a cartel covering the bulk of the world's oil supplies. The demand for oil is relatively price-inelastic and the supply is in the hands of a small number of countries. Severe price hikes since 1973 have not reduced the demand for oil significantly, though individual suppliers might be feeling the slight fall in world demand more than others. The low price elasticity of demand for oil and the high income elasticity of demand place OPEC in a powerful bargaining position. The combined

revenue to OPEC countries rose from $4·5 billion in 1966 to $15 billion in 1972 and is estimated to reach $56 billion in 1980.

Production costs of oil in the Middle East are less than 20 cents a barrel while in the North Sea the capital and operating costs are under $2·43 (with many fields under $2) a barrel. The world price would have to fall to near these figures to make North Sea Oil uncompetitive. Moreover, it would have to fall relatively soon because once the production expenditure has been met and the equipment installed it is technically difficult to stop the oil flowing. Thus, if the OPEC broke up, or oil was dumped on the world market at under $2 a barrel it might eliminate the expected returns from North Sea oil but it would not necessarily stop the oil coming ashore. Scotland, or Britain, would still be self-sufficient in oil irrespective of the price.

7. Independence with the oil balances would not be 'worth the candle' if a Scottish government pursued economic policies that meant the exchange rate for the Scottish pound against the English pound was allowed to double; if an oil-financed consumer boom was experienced, based on cheap imports to the detriment of domestic goods and services; if the rising exchange rate made Scottish exports completely uncompetitive; if Scottish productivity did not improve; if unemployment increased as the manufacturing sector accelerated its decline. In these circumstances the oil would be dissipated with a higher standard of living, higher unemployment and contraction of the export sector.

8. (a) Regional policy is based on distributing economic growth to the poorer regions. It requires both direction and incentives. If the economy is in recession, with little expansion anywhere, there is little to distribute and a wider area to distribute what is available. Scotland's industrial structure will be replaced over a longer time-span, with regional policy acting as a brake on the decline.

(b) Devolution without major economic powers to the Assembly will mean a continuation of central Regional Policy as above, with, perhaps, some political response to the Assembly in the form of a designated proportion of the oil revenues for Scottish re-investment. The main problem of regional policy remains: reconciling regional needs to expand with macro-stabilization requirements to contain national expansion with the constraints of UK balance payments, inflation and capacity.

(c) Independence, nominally at least, removes the latter constraint. It enables a regional expansion to take place, and a faster growth in net investment to replace declining industries with jobs and products. It brings about a real transfer of resources from England's manufacturing base to Scotland under the direction of Scottish political interests.

The main difference between them all is in the degree to which the resource transfer is controlled by either the centre or the region.

9. If the exchange value of the British pound falls this has two effects: it raises the prices of imports and reduces the price of exports in foreign currency terms. This can be said to benefit Scotland to the extent that it enables less efficient manufacturing industry to remain competitive with imported goods flowing into Britain and with competing goods on world export markets. In so far as imports to Scotland (and Britain) are price-inelastic in demand, the devaluation in the British pound raises the cost of imports (worsens the balance of payments). As exports are price-elastic overseas, through severe competition, the value of exports has to rise to compensate for the increase in the value of imports. If Scottish imports form a high proportion of the content of exports (e.g. Canadian grain in Scottish whisky) the increase in price due to devaluation-induced import price increases will work against the fall in price due to devaluation-induced export price falls. If imports form a high proportion of consumption, devaluation reduces the standard of living.

A rise in the Scottish exchange rate produces the opposite effects. Whether Scottish industry is better or worse off will depend on the rate of growth achieved, the relative proportion of industry that is import/export dependent, and the net effect on the trade balance.

10. At or near full employment, unless other measures are taken, consumer demand will begin to spill over into imports of consumer goods and services from the rest of the world, including England. If Scottish productivity remained in the same relationship to that of other manufacturing countries as at present imports would expand at the expense of domestic production and unemployment would increase. If that continued, the result would be substantial unemployment in Scottish industry, a high level of imports of consumer goods and services financed by an oil-based welfare state, both racing against the depletion of the oil resources in the North Sea.

The Scottish government should regard the oil as a capital asset to be transformed into other capital assets, i.e. into gross domestic fixed capital formation, with a view to re-equipping and expanding the manufacturing sector in order to raise manpower productivity to competitive levels. It should not regard it as a means to increasing private or public consumption. It should find a way of using the oil revenues in both the interests of its own economic development and the separate economic interests of its neighbour, England.

11. In this author's view it is, but it does presuppose a political environment in which it can be implemented. Issues to be resolved include: the sharing out of the oil revenues (the Scottish National Party want 100 per cent Scottish control; the Scottish Labour Party 30 per cent;

the Labour Party (Scottish Council), the Scottish Conservatives and the Scottish Liberals regard the oil as British); the terms under which each government can draw on the joint account; the fiscal rate of exchange of oil revenues for sterling; the disposal of sterling deposits on direct imports from England and indirect exports to developing countries; and the reciprocal agreement on English coal deposits.

12. Experience of Ireland since independence, up to the admission of Ireland and Britain to the EEC in 1972, was an illustration of the limitations of independence for different economic policies. Experience in the EEC suggests that there is scope for different policies, if only in the negative sense that member countries face different problems. Completely dissimilar policies between Scotland and England are probably limited by the substantial trading relationship and mutual consultation would be essential if changes were proposed that were likely to affect a neighbour.

13. It is also a fact that the coal reserves of England exceed by a wide margin the oil and gas reserves in the North Sea and once the oil is exhausted (around 2040) an entirely different energy situation will exist between the two countries (McRae, 1976). This prospect must act as an incentive for a Scottish government to negotiate a mutually advantageous and generous settlement with England, perhaps agreeing to a proportion of the oil going directly into English control in exchange for a commitment to devise a similar arrangement regarding English coal after 2000.

14. If it transpires that the joint account arrangement still provides Scotland with a surplus of sterling which it cannot use to acquire physical assets (because it has reached its absorption limit) or acquire control of current assets (because it has acquired all it wants or that is available) or which it cannot re-lend to the English government (because England has borrowed back all it thinks is prudent to borrow) what should it do? It has two choices in these circumstances. It can use the surplus sterling to acquire assets in England – net foreign investment –in much the same way that the Arabs have been doing with their oil revenues. This will add to Scotland's net property income from abroad in future years when it may be more convenient to carry out economic programmes than it is at present. It could also use some of these funds to give or loan abroad to developing countries who would be required only to spend them in Scotland on purchasing goods and services to assist their own development programmes. This would extend some of the benefits of North Sea oil to the Third World.

Savings in the United Kingdom

TEACHER'S NOTES

These notes are intended to provide more recent comments and data on the level of saving in relation to income. A comparison is also made with financial institutions in other countries. The personal savings ratio is examined over recent years and National Savings are investigated in the light of the reaction to the Page Report. Further suggestions are also made regarding rectification of the so-called savings scandal.

Savings and the Economy

In official Government statistics, saving by the personal sector is usually quoted on a gross basis and as the difference between total personal income and total current expenditure. Net saving, however, is calculated by allowing for stock appreciation and capital consumption: the latter cannot be identified through financial transactions and is an imputed calculation. As well as the examples of 'residual' calculations of savings, it is noteworthy that saving is essentially concerned with the acquisition of financial assets. The two figures, however, do not tally but the marked increase in personal savings cannot be disputed. An OECD Report in the late 1960s on Capital Markets indicated that the difference between the 'residual' calculation and 'identified' savings is due to both statistical errors and omissions but any correction, the Report suggests, would probably lead to an increase in the personal saving element.

The pattern of saving over the years 1965–75 is indicated in Table 3.5 extracted from the *National Income Blue Book*. Total personal income less United Kingdom taxes on income, national insurance, etc. contributions, transfers abroad (net) and taxes paid abroad equals personal disposable income.

The total funds at the disposal of the personal sector are obtained by the addition to gross saving of all personal borrowing, the proceeds of the sale of all stocks and shares and, of course, the 'unidentified' items. The latter component, except for 1972, has been a significant part of the overall total. Much of this sum could arise from the trade credit extended to customers by companies and hire purchase debt of private firms.

A comparison of the main savers in recent selected years reveals the trends shown in Table 3.6. The acquisition of assets has shown a fairly consistent and upward trend since the early 1960s and a dramatic increase

Table 3.5 The Personal Sector (£m.)

	1965	1966	1967	1968	1969	1970	1971	1972	1973	1974	1975
Personal disposable income	25,074	26,665	27,798	29,701	31,663	34,766	38,454	44,229	50,954	60,295	73,727
Saving	2,229	2,444	2,370	2,393	2,561	3,122	3,289	4,513	5,910	8,463	10,354
Savings as a percentage of disposable income	8·9	9·2	8·5	8·0	8·1	9·0	8·6	10·2	11·6	14·0	14·0
Personal disposable income at 1970 prices	31,506	31,208	32,661	33,274	33,539	34,766	35,545	38,311	40,650	41,427	41,153
Total Personal Income	30,083	32,190	33,840	36,463	31,113	43,323	47,744	54,228	62,775	75,850	95,700

in 1973. The main outlets have been the banks, building societies, life and pension funds. The remarkable growth of bank deposits since 1971 corresponds very closely to the new era of greater competition for the banks in attracting deposits fostered by the introduction of *Competition and Credit Control* in September 1971. The increase was also partly due to a transfer of funds from more risky areas and also to the uncertainty and depression in the stock market.

Table 3.6 UK Saving 1958 to 1973 (£m., net of stock appreciation and depreciation)

Year	Total	Personal Sector	%	Companies	%	Public Corporations	%	Central & Local Government	%
1958	1,853	213	11	1,405	76	−209	−11	444	24
1963	2,609	1,003	38	1,491	57	−64	−2	179	7
1968	3,791	1,325	35	1,052	28	−159	−4	1,573	41
1973	3,946	2,714	69	1,148	29	−756	−19	840	21

Source: 'Long term saving and finance: savings and the economy', *Barclays Bank Review*, February. 1975, p. 11.

The growth of the life assurance and pension funds has been less volatile than the banking sector. They cater essentially for long-term contractual saving and comprise the largest sector of the market for savings. At the end of 1973 the total accumulated investments of the life assurance funds amounted to £21,058 million compared to total holdings of £17,709 million and £10,450 million for the building societies and National Savings Banks respectively. Total investment by the pension funds (including public and private sector schemes) at the end of 1973 amounted to £10,593 million.[1]

Savings Institutions in Europe, Japan and the United States

In Europe, the scope of savings banks ranges from single deposit, interest-bearing and withdrawal facilities, to an almost complete banking service. There is a basic two-tier structure of savings banks in Europe, local or regional savings banks administered by private bodies and the centrally organized savings banks with a nationwide sphere of influence. There is a strong movement towards centralization. In the Netherlands mergers are planned to reduce the number of savings banks from 120 to 10–12 large institutions. In the UK the merger movement began in 1974 after the publication of the 1973 Page Report. The Trustee Savings Banks were to agree to reduce their numbers from 72 to 15 regional banks and no longer act as an official channel for National Savings. The TSB established their own central bank in November 1973, functioning as an ordinary commercial bank and as a clearing centre for the Trustee Savings Banks. There has also been more competition between the savings banks and other financial institutions in recent years. Savings banks in Europe have thus become more akin to commercial banks in their efforts to recruit funds and make loans and invest in areas other than the public sector. Stimulated by economies of scale and changes in banking regulations, a merger movement has taken place, which despite interruption in the pattern of savings in response to inflation, is likely to lead to a long-term strengthening in the foundations of savings banks.[2]

In Japan, there are trust banks, which along with the three long-term credit banks, provide the major source of long-term financing for large-scale industry and trade. The war, however, the inflation which followed, and the drastic changes in property distribution severely damaged the trust business. In 1948 the Government assisted them by allowing them to conduct ordinary banking business. There are now seven trust banks and one city bank with a trust division. In 1972 these banks accounted for nearly 30 per cent of all bank loans financing capital outlays by industry and trade. Since 1973, however, they have been severely hit by a tight monetary policy. Efforts have been made to reduce costs through modernization and increased efficiency but the vulnerability of the trust banks in times of economic recession has led to increasing pressure for them to merge with the city banks which have been aggressively expanding overseas.[3]

In the United States there are two main savings institutions, Savings and Loan associations and Mutual Savings Banks. Both have recently been squeezed owing to the vulnerability of their maturity structure in a time of rising interest rates. Their liabilities (to depositors) are in practice due on demand while their assets (largely home mortgages) are long-term. Ability to compete effectively against market interest rates is, therefore, severely limited because assets are tied up in mortgages contracted at lower interest rates. Furthermore, in the United States mortgages are a genuine fixed-interest long-term contract. The dilemma faced by the thrift institutions in times of rising interest rates is clear; if rates paid to depositors are not raised, net inflows of funds fall and illiquidity threatens, while if those rates are increased, profitability declines. In addition there are rigidities on the liabilities side of the balance sheet which derive from the influence of state using restrictions on the payment of interest. The result has been an outflow of funds from the thrift institutions in favour of other financial intermediaries. Since these thrift institutions are the main source of mortgage finance, it is clear why housing construction in the United States has for many years followed a trend opposite to the general movement of the economy, expanding in periods of economic slack and contracting in periods of economic expansion.[4]

The Personal Savings Ratio

The personal savings ratio measures the proportion of total personal disposable income which is not spent by the consumer. In recent years the UK personal savings ratio has shown a marked increase; rising from 8·9 per cent in 1971 to 12·7 per cent in 1974 and to 13·8 per cent in the first half of 1975. It has been suggested that the recent very high ratios are probably due in part to the rapid increase in nominal incomes in the latter part of 1974 but they may also be related to general uncertainty and to precautionary motives associated with rapidly rising prices and unemployment. Falling real asset values could also be a factor. The longer-term picture is illustrated in the diagram below for the period 1955–74. The underlying trend has clearly been upwards but between 1960–1 and 1972–4 there were particularly rapid increases. Between 1955–9 the personal savings ratio averaged 4·5 per cent a year, rising to 7·7 per cent a year in the period 1960–4. A further small rise in the second half of the 1960s was followed by a 10·6 per cent average for 1970–4.[5]

According to a research paper written by J. C. Townend in the *Bank of England Quarterly Bulletin*, the exceptionally high rate of personal saving between 1973–6 can only be partly explained by the equations normally used to determine and predict consumers' expenditure. Evidence was found to support the view that the value of liquid assets held by the personal sector, when adjusted for the effects of inflation, has had a significant effect on the volume of spending during the period, and was responsible for a large part of the unforeseen rise in saving since 1973. Some weaker evidence indicated that during a period of rapid inflation, expectations of price changes might lag behind actual changes, and that consumer resistance might then result in less expenditure and higher saving. Other possible theories were tested including the uncertainty of employment prospects and future standards of living, and reductions in the value of illiquid wealth associated with the general weakness of financial and property markets in 1974 and the early part of 1975.

Empirical results show that consumption patterns change relatively slowly in response to movements in income, an observation which is consistent with a number of theories. Milton Friedman's 'permanent income hypothesis' for example, suggests that people tend to adjust their consumption patterns only to those variations in current income which they expect to persist. A second theory relates inertia or lack of awareness to the long delay before spending adjusts to income. A third stresses force of habit with expenditure determined by previous experience rather than current earnings. Equations derived from these theories produced satisfactory results in the 1960s and early 1970s but more recently they

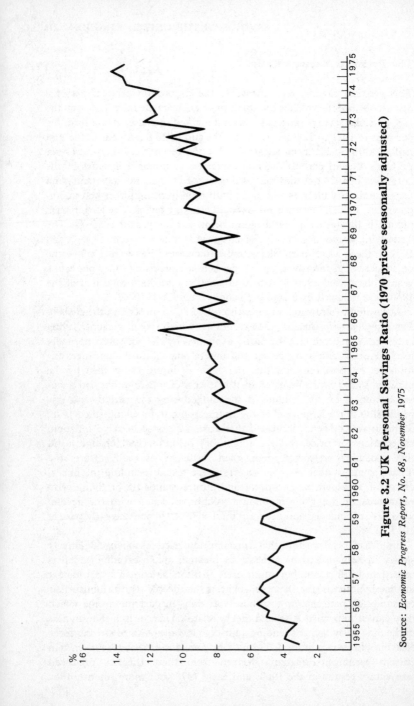

Figure 3.2 UK Personal Savings Ratio (1970 prices seasonally adjusted)

Source: *Economic Progress Report, No. 68, November 1975*

have overestimated spending and understated the rise in the saving ratio.[6]

Considerable support is given in the *Bulletin* to the theory of John Forsyth, chief economist of the merchant bankers Morgan Grenfell. If holdings of liquid assets fall in relation to disposable income, an attempt is made to restore some of the shortfall by saving a higher proportion of current income. The inclusion of the stock of liquid assets led to a substantial improvement in the statistical properties of the equation in terms of good fit and predictive performance reducing forecasting errors by half. The results suggest that as the rate of inflation moderates, the saving ratio should decline.

A report in the *Financial Times* by Anthony Harris commented: 'An advance of this scale in the accuracy of forecasting is a rare event in economic research and goes far to explain the evident excitement of the Bank's economists over their finding and their willingness to challenge so radically the figures used by other forecasters.'[7] Several explanations of this behaviour may be suggested; that peoples' spending is determined by the size of their bank balance, as well as by their income; that people have an intuitive feeling about the appropriate balance between assets and income; or that the main pressure is exerted by those who are in short-term debt to their banks or others. The research also shows that net rather than gross assets (net of short-term debt to banks and hire purchase companies) provides the explanation of savings behaviour and that, when consumers do decide to save more, they cut spending on food, clothing and services rather than on durable goods such as cars. The Bank's economists believe that the fall in saving may be slow to appear in Britain because, although inflation is slowing down, the stock of liquid assets remains at very low levels, about 20 per cent below the normal level for the 1960s and this will take time to rebuild.[8]

National Savings Since the Page Report

In anticipating the publication of the Page Report on 23 June 1973, *The Economist* expected several controversial recommendations regarding the role of voluntary workers, the future of the Trustee Savings Banks, and whether National Savings offer a fair return on savers' money. It is clear, however, that the Treasury has every incentive to keep rates of interest in National Savings as low as possible in order to keep down the cost of Government borrowing. A rise in National Savings rates can have unfortunate effects on other savings institutions, in particular the building societies. When this happened in 1973 the building societies had to be given a temporary Government grant of £25 million to keep their interest competitive.

The total net inflow to National Savings during 1975–6 was £783 million compared with £302·1 million in 1974–5 and £172·2 million in 1973–4. This was part of the general tendency to save a high proportion of disposable income but National Savings has no longer been the poor relation of other forms of saving. National Savings has offered relatively high rates of fixed interest on funds and savings accounts; attractive index-linked schemes; and premium bonds for those who wish to gamble.

It is instructive to investigate what has been done to implement Page's proposals. These were briefly that the Trustee Savings Banks should be made a third force in banking, standing between the National Savings Bank and the clearing banks. Secondly, that the range of National Savings Treasury securities should be simplified. Thirdly, that the National Savings Voluntary Movement should be wound up and finally that there should be some experiment in index-linking. The proposals on the Trustee Savings Banks and index-linking were taken up but not the other two.

The Trustee Savings Bank now has its central structure completed and is ready and willing to compete with the clearing banks but it has drifted away from the National Savings movement. It is perhaps unlikely to become a 'third force' because of its thin branch network in the southern part of England but it is very keen to become a 'social bank' for the individual rather than the commercial borrower.

Index-linking has been even more successful. The Index-linked Retirement Certificate has sold over £280 million with about 630,000 holders and Index-linked 'Save-As-You-Earn' has over 350,000 contracts and contributions running at £5 million per month. The main difficulty has been the intricacies of the schemes which has caused problems for investors and some Post Office staff.[9]

Page estimated that there were between 150,000 and 200,000 voluntary workers and he commented that it was difficult to calculate the extent of their financial contribution and the cost of raising the money and he questioned their aims and effectiveness. He recommended that the National Savings Stamp be abandoned.

Abolishing the role of the voluntary workers was rejected by the Government and they have been congratulated for their educational and social activities. The Savings Stamp, however, was to go by the end of 1976 and thus it has become necessary for the Community Group to find a new role in the general promotion of saving. There was great opposition to the disappearance of the stamp but it is recognized that the image of middle-class village ladies in flowery hats encouraging thrift in the lower classes must go. The National Savings Committee has stressed that Page had the wrong idea about voluntary workers. They were never 'woolly-minded do-gooders', but included professional people who often performed their National Savings functions as an inevitable part of their job.

One example was organizing SAYE deductions from the wage packets of employees. In support of the voluntary workers Mr Desmond Ashton-Jones of the National Savings Committee in 1974 has said: 'The voluntary savings movement remains one of the largest in the world and is the envy of many other nations in that it serves over 4·6 million men, women and children. . . . To provide freely such a service to 10 per cent of the population is no mean achievement.[10]

The revival of National Savings has thus been due partly to changing economic conditions and partly to Page's proposals. Problems still remain, however. There are still too many savings institutions in the UK competing for funds, encouraging one at the expense of another produces strains. The relationship of the National Savings Bank with Post Office Giro or even the Trustee Savings Bank is still uncertain. The relationship of the voluntary movement with the Department of National Savings is also unclear. The Committee for National Savings is responsible for publicity but the main resources of finance and staff are provided by the Department.

The Savings 'Scandal'

Dr John Foster of Glasgow University suggested in *The Guardian* that inflation is causing a tremendous shift in wealth and the real losers appear to be the non-tax-paying pensioner. He illustrates his ideas with building society shares and deposits because it is possible to be more precise about the impact of inflation on them than on other short-term savings. Building societies are non-profit-making to any losses incurred by savers and simultaneous gains by borrowers. They exist to lend for mortgages so the borrowers are clearly defined. In 1975 the average holding of building society savings was £17,467 and the rate of inflation was 19·9 per cent, which meant a loss of purchasing power of £3,476 million at average prices. After-tax interest rate was 7·5 per cent, so the real interest rate, allowing for the decline in the purchasing power of money was 12·2 per cent. Dr Foster calculates how much savers were losing from inflation by estimating what the interest rate would have been in the absence of serious inflation. He takes 2 per cent as a conservative estimate and shows that in 1974 there was a 14·4 per cent difference between the real rate paid and this non-inflation estimate. This represented a loss of £1,538 million at average prices in 1974. The losers are those whose building society savings exceed mortgage borrowing.

About 70 per cent of building society savings are held by the over-55 age group who hold only 3·5 per cent of mortgage borrowing. So as a group they incur about 66·5 per cent of the total losses due to inflation (£1,023 million at average prices in 1974). Correspondingly the under-55 age made an equal gain. That is a very serious situation for people who depend on such savings for their retirement years. It also tends to be the poorest of the aged who hold savings in this medium.

In terms of income, 20 per cent of building society savings are held by those paying no income tax but only between 1 and 4 per cent of mortgage borrowing. So the lowest income group incurs at least 16 per cent of the total losses due to inflation. Dr Foster states that as non-profit-making institutions, the building societies are uniquely placed to introduce the necessary reforms to protect their savers from inflation through the indexation of interest payments.[11]

In commenting on Dr Foster's article a Mr G. W. Green calculated rather differently. He stated that Dr Foster's assumptions were wrong and his arithmetic atrocious but he still managed to find approximately the right answer. Mr Green's calculation yielded a total loss to savers in 1974 of £1,764 million and he also commented that the 1975 figure of £3,000 million loss to savers was even more scandalous. He also disagreed with the suggestion of indexation of interest payments. He believed that this would attract more money into the societies and away from other more important sectors of the economy. As far as borrowers were concerned, many would be unable to pay a realistic rate of interest as this would always have to be slightly higher than the rate of inflation. In 1974 the interest would have been 21 per cent. Mr Green's remedy is a massive reduction in inflation and an extension of Government index-linked saving schemes and in particular an index-linked gilt-edged stock. This would not only protect savers but also help meet the public sector borrowing requirement.[12]

Mr Keir Hardman considered that Dr Foster's analysis was invalid on two counts. The first concerns his consideration of taxation. The tax paid on share accounts is an indirect decision by the saver to spend some of the income from his investment. The real comparison, according to Mr Hardman, should be made between 19·9 per cent inflation rate and the gross return paid by the building societies of 11 per cent. The net loss thus becomes 9 per cent rather than the 14·4 per cent loss suggested by Dr Foster.

The second point concerns the power of the building societies to set interest rates as they see fit. This is not the case in practice. The building societies adjust the interest rate as dictated by the pressures of the housing market so as to balance the funds lent to them with the cash they make available to borrowers.[13]

Mr Norman Griggs, Secretary-General, The Building Societies Association, comments that the association has given careful consideration to schemes for indexation but 'it would not seem practical for building societies to introduce indexation unilaterally' Any institution offering inflation-proofed savings at the present time would scoop the pool and it seems likely that indexation could only come about as part of a national plan embracing the whole economy.'[14]

REFERENCES

1. 'Long term saving and finance: savings and the economy'. *Barclays Bank Review*, February 1975, pp. 11–12.
2. 'Savings institutions: in Europe, Japan, United States', *Barclays Bank Review*, February 1975, pp. 5–8.
3. *ibid.*, pp. 8–9.
4. *ibid.*, pp. 9–10.
5. 'Personal savings', *Economic Progress Report*, No. 68, November 1975, p. 6.
6. J. C. Townend, 'The personal savings ratio', *Bank of England Quarterly Bulletin*, March 1976, pp. 53–73.
7. A. Harris, 'Rise in personal savings prompted by inflation', *Financial Times*, 11 March 1976.
8. *ibid.*
9. C. Hill, 'An end to the flowery hat image', *Financial Times*, 31 July 1976, p. 11.
10. Letter to *The Economist*, 17 August 1974.
11. Dr J. Foster, 'Real losers in the great savings scandal', *The Guardian*, 2 January 1976.
12. Letters to *The Guardian*, 6 January 1976.
13. *ibid.*
14. *ibid.*

FURTHER READING

The article by John Forsyth referred to in the case study is strongly recommended. The extensive survey on Savings by Brian Reading in *The Economist*, also referred to, is also suggested. *The Times* on 19 February 1976 issued a Special Report to mark the National Savings Movement's diamond jubilee.

Resources for Learning Ltd have issued in conjunction with the Economics Association two study kits called *Life Assurance: an industrial analysis* and *Building Societies and the Housing Market*. These are available from Lark Hill, Parsons Road, Bradford.

POINTS INTENDED TO BE RAISED FROM THE QUESTIONS

1. The main factors which influence the level of savings are:

   (a) The level of income. As income increases, so does the ability to save. The rich man or society spends a greater absolute sum but a smaller proportion of total income than the poor man or society.

   (b) Attitudes to saving. Thrift may be thought to be a virtue and thus more will be saved, as in Britain during the nineteenth century, or alternatively societies may be encouraged to consume almost as an end in itself as in Orwell's *1984*.

   (c) Financial institutions. Some economies have the advantage of many institutions for the safe deposit of savings which are widely known, easily accessible, and readily utilized by the people. In less developed societies such sophisticated institutions are rare and are inadequately understood by the majority of the people.

   (d) The rate of interest. Although there is some disagreement among economists about the importance of the rate of interest, it is clear that interest is the price paid for the sacrifice of current consumption. Other factors are also important such as habit, thrift, the psychological feeling of security with 'capital' in the bank. Furthermore a large proportion of saving is contractual. Many people save for a specific target such as an annual holiday. In all these cases the rate of interest will have little effect. It should also be emphasized that approximately half the total saving in the UK is accounted for by companies.

2. In the early 1950s, the largest savers were the self-employed, ploughing back savings into their own businesses. The 'managerial and technical' group came next in order, followed by the skilled manual workers. Clerical and sales staff and unskilled manual workers seemed to save very little. The 20 per cent of the population retired or unemployed tended to spend in excess of income, i.e. were considerable dis-savers. The study points out that estimates of the marginal propensity to save suggest that the marginal propensity of the self-employed is much higher than average, their saving being a third to a half of any increase in income. For managerial and technical groups, the marginal share of saving, though significant, is much less. As far as the retired section of the population is concerned, the rate to which they live on past saving, oddly enough, appears unrelated to their current income.

   By 1964 total savings accounted for approximately one-fifth of UK national income. Of this total, personal savings accounted for 30 per cent, central government, local authorities and public corporations 21 per cent but the largest single group, companies, accounted for 49 per cent. More recent figures indicate a significant increase in total savings to 25 per cent of national income. The proportion saved by the government largely depends on policy considerations. Thus the 29·7 per cent figure for central government saving in 1969 was due to a substantial budget surplus. In contrast, however, in 1972, the government was running a budget deficit, and its saving accounted for 10·8 per cent of the total. Personal savings took 33·9 per cent and company savings 40·5 per cent of total savings. For a comprehensive survey of recent statistics on saving and their relation to national income the *National Income Blue Book* should be consulted.

3. The Government has considerable influence on the level of saving and if it can encourage a higher level of saving, it is able to finance its expenditure without an excessive burden of taxation. Not only does saving help provide finance for the economy but it can be used as a regulator of personal consumption. The problem of what causes changes in the level of savings has baffled many economists. Note the comment of the Radcliffe Committee Report, 1959, quoted in the study. 'We have found no satisfactory explanation of the large changes that have taken place in the rate of private saving over the past ten years.' Periods of rapid growth of disposable income, however, tend to be followed by high levels of saving in the following year. There were also Government curbs on consumer demand in the years under discussion which tended to encourage saving. Taxation has an effect on the savings ratio and in particular direct taxation. The higher income groups have the greatest propensity to save so that any increase in income tax has a disproportionate effect on the savings ratio. Contractual savings assume great importance in Britain through life assurance and pension funds. Of the total increase in savings between 1962 and 1966 60 per cent was due to net increases in life assurance and superannuation schemes. This high rate of contractual savings has enabled the institutional investors to collect and distribute funds efficiently. Furthermore, contractual savings tend to be fairly insulated from the effects of short-run fluctuations in income. They are thus more stable.

4. The essential data to answer this question are those offered by Hicks in Tables 3.2, 3.3 and 3.4. Private and corporate savings in France appeared, for the time periods surveyed, to be slightly lower than in Britain. They were much higher in Germany. There was a marked difference between the three countries in respect of the importance of government savings. The figure was much smaller in Britain than in France with Germany having an even larger ratio.

If saving performance is examined from the point of view of the saver, that is, private income net of direct taxation, and the proportion of that 'disposable income' which is not consumed is calculated, the

French propensity to save appears lower than the British and far lower than the German. The major part of private saving in Britain, however, is the saving of companies (through undistributed profits), while in France and Germany, corporate saving is only a fraction of the total (25 per cent or less compared with UK's 40 per cent).

5. Lomax and Reading suggest that Britain's poor savings performance in the 1960s was due to our tax system and the increasing disincentive to saving over time. Professor Hill, on the other hand, implied that increased taxation might strengthen the economy. The table quoted in the study makes it clear that Britain's poor savings performance could not be explained by total taxes on incomes. The significant factor would seem to be the severity of the direct tax system on the higher levels of income and on the returns from saving. Thus the system takes a larger proportion as incomes rise, whether the rise is due to a real increase in income or merely reflects inflation. Sir John Hicks in the *Three Banks Review* in June 1968 points to the failure of industry when undertaking expansion, to make sufficient allowance for working capital. He comments that to maintain production at a high level, a more or less proportionate increase in stock and work in progress will be required to support it.

When Britain's savings figures are compared with France and Germany, private and corporate saving in Britain and France are on average about the same between 1960 and 1965, but the German figures are much higher. The most obvious difference is in Government saving (see Table 3.4) where the Germans have by far the largest proportion. This seems to have been achieved by large budget surpluses. The small proportion of government saving in Britain and the reliance of industry on investment finance from undistributed profits and government taxation policy have tended to diminish the contribution that might have been made from personal savings.

6. Note the comment by Harold Wincott in the *Financial Times* '. . . any further increase in taxation of either incomes or spending is largely if not entirely self-defeating, if only because people adjust their savings, rather than their living standards, to such increases'. He noted the impressive performance of the building societies while savings as a whole were much less so. The importance of contractual saving must also be emphasized. Both pension funds and life assurance grew during the period 1962–6. A significant fact was the fastest growing means of saving – the unit trust. Perhaps this indicated a desire for security with growth on the part of the saver.

Having dismissed the National Savings Movement as a means of stimulating saving, Mr Wincott turned to the private sector savings media, commenting that if a higher proportion of income could have been saved the crises could have been avoided, taxation could have been kept down, productive investment could have been increased and a better spread of wealth thereby achieved.

Mr Brian Reading in April 1968 proposed special three-year tax-free savings accounts voluntarily deducted with PAYE, which after three years could be transferred into the Post Office or other forms of saving. Lionel Barras suggested remission of tax payable under Schedule E by 10 per cent of the aggregate investments in recognized savings media. The Wider Share Ownership Council suggested 'thrift plans' where employees regularly subscribe to a trust for investment in approved media, plus shares in the company which employs them. Withdrawal would be permitted after three years. The Confederation of British Industry has suggested these ideas but has also proposed a link with the cost-of-living index. The National Savings Committee advocated a three-to five-year 'lock-up' fixed interest medium with an interest rate above current levels and a limit on the amounts invested.

With regard to contractual savings schemes, one interesting idea of Mr Tim Sainsbury's was to provide tax concessions varying with the state of the economy. Other schemes proposed involve anti-inflation devices, tax concessions on interest, or even on the principal, or a bonus at the end of the contractual period rather than tax concession. Several people suggested a nationwide contractual scheme to be incorporated within the PAYE system. Such a scheme was introduced in 1969, 'Save As You Earn', operated by the Department for National Savings, Trustee Savings banks and building societies.

7. Useful reference may be made here to the June 1971 edition of the Treasury *Economic Progress Report*. Between 1960 and 1970 the personal sector's share of savings, as a proportion of GNP, has remained very steady at an average of just over 6 per cent. Company saving, their undistributed income after tax, declined from 55 per cent of total saving in the late 1950s to 28 per cent in 1970. Public sector saving has varied considerably. It includes central government, public corporations and local authorities. A sample of figures over this period illustrates the variability: 1960, 16 per cent of total saving, 1965 25 per cent, 1968 35 per cent, 1970 45 per cent (central government 34 per cent, public corporations 7 per cent, local authorities 4 per cent). The share of public corporations and local authorities remained fairly steady during the period. The central government varies its rate of saving according to the amount of investment it wishes to finance, and to general economic policy considerations.

Within the category of personal savings there was a noticeably large increase in contractual saving and heavy sales of company and government securities. It would appear that the personal sector had switched from direct to indirect holding of these securities.

8. The British saver appeared to believe that inflation of over 25 per cent

was merely a passing phase and not a permanent change in the economic climate. He seemed to be willing to pay for security by losing a significant part of the value of his savings. *The Economist* calculated that the £112 billion of financial assets fell to £86 billion at end 1973 prices, but at mid-1975 prices the loss increases from £26 billion to £35 billion. The Treasury in April 1975 indicated its uncertainty concerning the high level of saving in a period of rapid inflation. It suggested that savings behaviour might be influenced not just by changes in the level of income but also people's feelings about their stock of assets. The most interesting, and seemingly accurate theory was propounded by Mr John Forsyth. His thesis was that the amount people save is largely determined by the ratio between their liquid assets and their disposable income. Thus people spend more of their income when they have substantial holdings of liquid assets in banks, building societies and so on. When income rises, this stock of liquidity declines in relation to income unless it is replaced out of current saving. The theory accurately forecasts the actual level of savings in the eighteen months to September 1975, a much better forecast than the purely income-determined relationship. In the 1970s, the growth of incomes rose far more rapidly than that of liquid assets. The savings ratio rose as people found their assets dwindling in real terms. The relationship works much better than the 'permanent income' hypothesis of Milton Friedman. This theory states that people have strong underlying expectations about their standard of living and its progress. When income grows faster than these expectations, the surplus is saved; if it falls behind, they maintain expected living standards by dipping into past savings. The theory was appropriate in explaining the high savings ratio in 1974 when personal incomes rose faster than prices but could not explain the persistence of high savings ratios in 1975 when real personal incomes had fallen.

9. A substantial increase in total saving has been accomplished by a lower rate of industrial investment. Conventional economic analysis indicates that people save more out of higher incomes but not that they will save more as they become poorer. This is what led *The Economist* to refer to the 'new deflationary gap'. The imbalance between saving and investment has not been surprising. The reasons for higher levels of saving have already been advanced. The low rate of investment is understandable with inflation and high interest rates, slump and lower returns on the existing capital stock, and depressing anticipated returns on prospective investment.

In using Budget deficits in a period of slumpflation in order to deal with the deflationary gap unemployment is likely to be increased rather than reduced. The inflationary spiral is also likely to be given another twist with the increased Budget deficit feeding the money supply when real output is static. There is also the problem that wage push inflation may encourage people to save more and persuade businessmen to invest less, so that a larger government deficit could make the deflationary gap bigger rather than fill it. The effects of additional inflation on savings and investment behaviour could outweigh the demand effects of increased government spending.

Value Added Tax in the United Kingdom

TEACHER'S NOTES

INTRODUCTION

These further notes are intended as additional material primarily for the teacher but they may be of use to students undertaking an in-depth study of value added tax. Accordingly, there are three main sections in this material, subdivided as follows: Firstly there is further subject material which discusses macroeconomic theory and developments, and then developments in the EEC. Secondly there are suggestions for further reading and source material. Finally there are points intended to be raised from the questions.

FURTHER SUBJECT MATERIAL.

MACROECONOMIC THEORY AND DEVELOPMENTS

VAT has a macroeconomic importance as it is part of the general structure of indirect taxation in the United Kingdom, indirect taxation being a main influence upon consumption expenditure and also a part of the governmental accounts. Accordingly, Keynesian analysis focuses upon the role of taxation in the determination of short-run national income and hence employment. In recent years the success of Keynesian demand management techniques and analysis has come under some attack. Nevertheless a Keynesian approach has various avenues of development.

It is not difficult to indicate in what direction changes in indirect taxation, via value added tax, will affect national income. It is more difficult to quantify the relationship. Simple Keynesian manipulation of the multiplier can yield some arithmetic results. Similarly models of the economy can be constructed incorporating more complex multipliers. This might involve the construction of several consumption functions for differing income groups. It is highly likely that differing income groups will have differing consumption determinants. Alternative theories of consumption might be explored, for example Duesenberry, Friedman and Modigliani. The effect of demand changes on equilibrium national income can be extended by consideration of the monetary markets.

How value added tax changes affect general price levels too is far from understood. In theory this depends on the market structure and behavioural assumptions in the theory of the firm. In practice VAT has been a factor in 'VATflation'. *Barclays Bank Review*, February 1973, showed the increase in the price level in the member countries of the EEC that had VAT for significant lengths of time (Table 4·9). However, one cannot

Table 4.9

Country	Introduction of VAT	Quarterly increases in Consumer Price (%)	
		3 months prior to VAT	3 months after VAT
Denmark	3 July 1967	1·67	6·56
France[1]	1 January 1968	0·89	1·77
Germany	1 January 1968	0·00	0·99
Netherlands[2]	1 January 1969	1·60	4·72
Luxemburg	1 January 1970	0·68	2·35
Belgium	1 January 1971	0·54	1·39

Notes: 1. A partial VAT had been in existence since April 1954.
   2. VAT was partially introduced on 1 June 1968.
Source: 'Vatflation' *Barclays Bank Review*, February 1973, p. 14.

attribute the difference in pre- and post-VAT rates of inflation solely to VAT. Similarly figures presented by C. M. Allan (*see* 'Points intended to be raised,' to question 5) support the view that the precise effects of indirect taxation, and so value added tax, are difficult to predict. Taxation structures differ from country to country and this influences both the formulation, and the outcome, of macroeconomic policy. (Table 4.10).

Table 4.10 Distribution of Tax Revenues and Social Security Contributions as Percentage of Total Taxation in 1973

	Taxes on Income		Taxes on Expenditure	Social Security contributions ( )=employees' contribution
	Households	Corporations		
(A)				
Belgium	28·7	8·4	31·9	31·0
Germany	38·8	4·2	35·7	31·2 (19·7)
Italy	18·0	4·9	36·9	40·2
Japan	25·8	21·6	34·3	18·4
United Kingdom	31·5	8·9	42·9	16·7 (8·8)
(B)				
Denmark	55·7	2·9	38·8	2·5
France	11·6	6·4	43·6	38·4 (28·4)
Netherlands	28·2	6·8	26·9	38·2 (19·3)
Norway	—	—	38·3	29·3
Sweden	42·0	3·0	35·1	20
United Kingdom	33·1	10·0	40·6	16·3 (8·5)
United States	31·6	13·1	31·3	24·0

Note: Countries in group B have had calculations based upon the new United Nations system of accounts (SNA), those in table A on the basis of the old SNA.
Source: 'International comparisons of taxes and social security contributions 1969–73', *Economic Trends*, December 1975, p. 98.

The balance of payments effects of value added tax are superficially persuasive in that imports bear the tax whereas exports do not. However, value added tax is not primarily used to adjust the balance of payments. This is a question of exchange rate policy and monetary and fiscal policy.

The other side of taxation and hence of VAT is its part in the governmental accounts. More general models of the economy incorporate a monetary sector and stress the importance of the public sector borrowing requirement, crudely the excess of government spending over revenue, in expanding the money supply. Whether increased taxation is used, for example, to increase government spending or to reduce the PSBR, will decidely affect the impact of the change on national income. If government spending is increased in line with rises in taxation revenue, this will lead to balanced budget multiplier effects. If the increased taxation is not used for this purpose, how the PSBR is reduced will alter the money supply accordingly. VAT must thus be considered both for its primary Keynesian effects upon consumption and for its part in any economic readjustment that the government may make.

The timing of VAT changes is also problematical. The multiplier effects take time to work themselves out (the various rounds or stages of the multiplier). It may be that the government considers only the first three rounds of the multiplier process as its time horizon. This further complicates the calculation of indirect tax changes necessary to achieve a given national income change.

Developments in the EEC

Events in Brussels have occurred at a renewed pace during 1976. The early belief that the EEC could achieve economic union is back in fashion, at least in part. A series of meetings in 1976 under the EEC Commissioner for Fiscal Affairs, Sig. Cesidio Guazzaroni, and the Dutch President of the Fiscal Council, Mr Wilhelm Duisenberg has produced significant advances. From 1 January 1978 national contributions to the EEC kitty will be stopped to be replaced by direct financing, known in the EEC as its 'own resources' plan. These resources are to be import levies and customs duties, which it already collects and which accounted for 60 per cent of EEC revenue in 1975, and by a share of national VAT revenues, up to the equivalent of a 1 per cent rate across the EEC.

Given this latter change it is essential that all member states collect VAT on a fair proportion of their economic activities. At present countries differ in the products falling into the net for VAT, the rates at which VAT is levied and the proportions of GNP that are spent on consumption. This latter point is important since the new system will mean that countries which consume a high fraction of GNP (like the UK) will pay relatively more and those which consume a lower fraction (like Germany) relatively less. Attempts to align the impact of VAT have involved a range of issues:

exempt goods, allowable inputs, small business threshold, the period of transition.

On 16 December 1976 a package was agreed upon in principle, that will, over a five-year transition period ending in 1983, produce a broadly common base for VAT throughout the Community. Agreement was reached on the broad issue of which goods were to be exempt. Zero-rated goods need not be phased out over the transitional period and can be continued indefinitely. Nevertheless, zero-rated goods will have to pay the notional 1 per cent rate. The UK, for example, will have to pay a notional 1 per cent rate on such items as food and childrens' clothing. The question of the turnover below which businesses are not liable was not settled. In the UK this threshold is £5,000 per year and has been since 1973. There is some pressure to raise this threshold, and the EEC limit is unlikely to be lower than this, and may well be periodically revised to take account of inflation. Whilst several countries tabled reservations about certain technical items and certain issues do remain unsolved, Guazzaroni was hailing the December meeting as so big a step forward in Community development as direct elections to the European Parliament.

FURTHER READING

Books

P. Bohm, *Social Efficiency*, Macmillan, 1973.

B. Crick and W. A. Robson (eds.), *Taxation Policy*, Pelican 1973, especially Chapter 13 by D. Stout.

J. Driscoll *et al.*, *The Implications of VAT*, Kluiver Harrap, 1972.

D. C. L. Johnstone, 'The VAT in the UK: Some of the Administrative Problems of its Introduction', in International Tax Conference, Singapore, 1974.

C. K. Sullivan, *The Tax on Value Added*, Columbia University Press, 1965.

A. Tait, *Value Added Tax*, McGraw Hill, 1972.

P. B. Warren, *A Businessman's Guide to VAT*, Gower Press, 1972.

The Report of the Committee on Turnover Taxation (the 'Richardson Committee'), Cmnd 2300, 1964.

Articles

'More indirect taxes', *The Economist*, 28 January 1961.

'Requiem for TVA', *The Economist*, 14th March 1964.

'The development of purchase tax', *Midland Bank Review*, August 1969.

S. S. Surrey, 'VAT: the case against' and D. T. Smith, 'VAT: the case for', *Harvard Business Review*, November–December 1970.

E. G. Horsman, 'Britain and value added taxation', *Lloyds Bank Review*, January 1972.

POINTS INTENDED TO BE RAISED FROM THE QUESTIONS

Accepting that the ten questions are, in the main, wide-ranging and questions of the essay type we have indicated in the answers below only those main points which could be included on the basis of the case study material.

1. It depends on the nature and size of the business. For a small business-man, turnover below £5,000 per year, it could be advantageous to be exempt as this eliminates the necessity for making any VAT returns. The costs of making such returns, for example the opportunity cost of lost production, may be high. The disadvantage is that no refund can be claimed for inputs bearing VAT. This may not be too disadvantage-ous if VAT can be fully shifted on to the consumer via price increases. For a larger business, zero rating means that VAT levied on inputs may be claimed back and the final stage of production and distribution bears no VAT.

2. Cascade type taxes are variants on a tax levied on some or all of the stages in the production and distribution chain. It is a cumulative tax, unlike VAT. The experience of European countries using cascade type taxes has been that companies tend to integrate vertically. This reduces the number of tax stages and hence the amount of tax paid. Vertically integrated companies would thus have lower tax bills (and hence prices?), than non-integrated companies. Governments found themselves having to pass further legislation to offset this. Further disadvantages are that certain cascade taxes did not differentiate between consumption and investment goods, i.e. the tax base was over-general; also that exported goods were difficult to rebate because of the complexity of calculation of tax content. One positive advantage of cascade taxes is that a low rate of tax raises a large amount of revenue (*see* table in text and use other rates on it).

3. The EEC is an attempt to create a single economic block within which free trade, movement of factors of production and common economic policies take place. One aspect of this must be the adoption of a com-mon system of indirect taxation (the so called Sixth Directive of the Treaty of Rome). Firstly, this will enable the EEC to become self-financing in 1978. Secondly, differing indirect tax rates affect the trading flows between member nations. If there are differing tax bases and/or tax rates and/or regulations on rebates then export prices will

not reflect costs of production. Comparative advantage theory will then be distorted.

4. The single rate of VAT was felt to be an inadequate tool of economic management. A rise in a single-rate VAT system might be regressive in nature. Multiple-rate systems mean that differing products, and hence consumers, are affected by differential changes in rates. The most obvious grouping is between essential goods and services, and less essential goods and services (luxury goods), though other groups might include imported products, for example. Thus, consumption spending in general can be cut more easily and equitably or consumption spending on imports might be cut similarly. Multiple rates are thus an improved tool of economic management. Secondly, multiple rates enable governments to raise revenue quickly by having products which are highly price-inelastic, in the higher rating. Multiple rates violate the principle of neutrality but may be more equitable in operation.

5. Direct taxation changes will affect the multiplier process at an earlier stage than indirect taxation changes. Thus an equivalent direct taxation change will have a higher multiplier value than an indirect taxation change. It is probably easier to calculate a multiplier value for direct taxation changes as the marginal propensity to consume of the income groups affected may be easy to estimate. In contrast, indirect taxation changes alter consumption patterns of all consumers and the effects are thus more difficult to forecast. Allan gives an illustrative example (Table 4.11). Income tax charges and taxation on specific goods with well-known and inelastic demand are easier to estimate than general indirect taxation changes.

Table 4.11 Miscalculations of Revenue by Taxes, UK, 1951–63 inclusive

	Error percentage of estimated revenue
Oil duties	1·9
Tobacco duties	1·9
Income tax	2·3
Alcohol duties	2·9
Surtax	4·1
Profits tax	5·9
Purchase tax	6·4
Protective duties	11·8
Stamp duty	13·8

Source: C. M. Allan, *op. cit.*

The timing of direct versus indirect taxation is, however, very different. Direct taxation change takes some time, possibly one year or more, to plan and implement and is a relatively inflexible tool. Indirect taxation changes can be introduced, via the regulator, and become effective in a much shorter period, say a quarter year. The full multiplier effects of both may not however be considered or ever achieved.

6. The efficiency of collection can be measured by the amount of real revenue raised per taxman for the two taxes. Purchase tax was more efficient on this basis. However, the VAT system does raise more revenue and it may be that taxation is a decreasing returns industry, i.e. efficiency is bound to decrease. Secondly, figures on evasion under the two UK systems are ill-defined, though there may be a priori grounds for believing VAT to have a greater capacity for evasion.

7. Within a static model of an economy, the change would lead to a reduction in the equilibrium level of income and a readjustment of consumer spending between products. It would lead to a rise in the general level of prices, the amount depending on the construction of the Retail Price Index. The change would be regressive in nature, affecting all income groups in a broadly similar way. As a practical proposition for the UK, it might lead to a weakening of the current prices and incomes restraint and so wage claims might result. This in turn might increase inflation.

8. This is a speculative question, though informed speculation is possible. Given the feeling that direct taxation in the UK has reached some limit and that tax harmonization in the EEC will continue, then VAT will become a much more important tax. The yield from VAT may well rise considerably, multiple rates may well become entrenched and the movement of products into particular ratings will depend on the outcome of EEC negotiations.

9. Figure 4.3 illustrates the effect of imposing VAT, or increasing the rate of VAT, on a particular product. Note the disproportionate shift in the supply line, as VAT is an ad valorem tax. The initial equilibrium in this market is at I, with price OE and quantity traded OB. Initial consumer surplus is area EIJ, and initial producer surplus is area CEI, i.e. the area above the market price up to the demand line, and the area below the market price down to the supply line. After the tax change, equilibrium is restored at point G, with price rising to OF and quantity traded falling to OA. Consumer surplus changes to FGJ and producer surplus changes to DFG. The loss of consumer surplus in thus area EIGF, and producer surplus lost is (CEI-DGF). The revenue raised by the government is quantity of product sold times the value of the tax at equilibrium; which is OA × FK. The value of consumer surplus loss, producer surplus loss and revenue raised will all alter depending on the shape of the demand and supply lines, i.e. their elasticity along their length. In general, revenue raised will rise if we have price inelastic demand.

10. Indirect taxation causes changes in the prices of products. Unless the

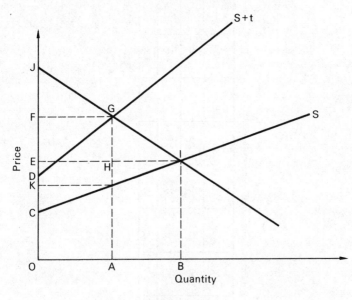

Figure 4.3

full effects of a tax can be foreseen, and this is unlikely even in a static general equilibrium economic model, there will be disproportionate changes in prices. This is the objective of Purchase Tax type taxes but not of broad-based Value Added type taxes. Differing income groups purchase differing bundles of products and so indirect taxation, if it leads to changes in relative prices, will be borne disproportionately by differing income groups. Thus income distribution is affected. Indirect taxation may be structured so as to be neutral with respect to income, progressive so as to fall more on higher income groups or regressive so as to fall more on lower income groups.

Evidence suggests that the United Kingdom indirect taxation system is broadly neutral (neither progressive nor regressive) in this respect. An article in December 1974 *Economic Trends* based upon data from the Family Expenditure Survey reached tentative conclusions on this issue. The study takes into account cash benefits (e.g. family allowances) and benefit in kind (such as per capita health and education services). For all taxes, direct and indirect, plus cash benefits the United Kingdom system was found to be mildly progressive and remarkably constant over a wide range. Whilst income tax, and the then surtax, are progressive, flat-rate social security contributions are mildly regressive as are indirect taxes as a whole (although over a wide range they tend to be proportional). Table 4.12 shows this.

Table 4.12 Selected Indirect Taxes as Percentage of Household Income per Year (for all households in sample 1973)

	Under £381	381—	461—	557—	674—	816—	987—	1194—	1446—	1749—	2116—	2561—	3099—	3750 +	Average Over Whole range
Local Rates	4·9	3·9	3·6	4·1	3·6	3·8	3·2	3·2	2·7	2·7	2·4	2·3	2·2	1·2	2·5
Tobacco Duties	2·6	3·0	2·7	2·6	3·6	3·3	3·6	4·0	3·5	3·2	3·0	2·8	2·4	1·2	2·6
PT/VAT	1·6	2·1	2·0	2·0	2·4	3·1	2·5	3·0	2·7	2·8	2·9	3·0	3·0	3·3	2·9

Source: *Economic Trends*, December 1974.

Economic Growth and Industrial Fluctuations in the United Kingdom and West Germany in the Last Two Decades

TEACHER'S NOTES

For any government interested in the well-being of its subjects, growth is an undisputed objective, given that well-being is correlated with the volume of production. The existence of this correlation, however, has more recently been disputed. Economists taking this view argue that growth can burden society with excessive social costs which outweigh the benefits of additional output and consumption – the costs of pollution, resource depletion and the unequal levels of economic development have been particularly emphasized in this debate.

Nevertheless, it is now more than twenty years since the achievement of a high and stable rate of economic growth became an acknowledged macroeconomic objective of the UK government. In a White Paper[1] published in 1956, it was declared that, 'the Government is pledged to foster conditions in which the nation can, if it so wills, realise its full potentialities for growth in terms of production and living standards'. This commitment has been continuously reaffirmed by successive governments since that date. The Conservative Government of 1962 recognized a need to promote a faster rate of growth in the UK, and proceeded to establish the National Economic Development Council which sought to determine the obstacles to growth and to evaluate the means of improving: 'economic performance, competitive power, and efficiency'.[2] But Conservative governments were not alone in the pursuit of growth; the National Plan put forward by the Labour Government of 1965, was intended to be a blue print for providing: 'the basis for greater economic growth'. The UK's balance of payments and sterling problems of the mid-1960s (*see* Table 5.1 in the case study) soon made the intended 25 per cent growth over the five-year period up to 1970 irrelevant. Despite the 1967 devaluation of sterling, which was intended to give a stimulus to British exports and to reduce the external constraint on the internal development of the economy, and the concern for fostering growth, the UK has met with little success – where success is judged on the basis of international comparisons of growth performance. Indeed most studies indicate that the UK has continuously found itself in the relegation zone of the international league tables for economic growth.[3]

Not of course that international comparisons of growth rates are an ideal basis for assessment. The text in fact makes reference to the case for making comparison with an economy's growth potential or target rate of growth. Alternatively the comparison could be intertemporal rather than international. It is the case for instance that the UK's growth experience of the last two decades compared favourably with that of the earlier decades of this century. To interpret the UK's post-war performance as that of a mature economy with a relatively low growth potential is however either pessimistic for our prospects or unacceptable. Given the commonality of socio-economic structure and experience, it seems unlikely that the UK should achieve 'maturity' before West Germany and at a lower level of per capita RGNP. Increasing awareness of comparable living standards, especially within the European Economic Community, will make the need for optimism and a search for explanations more pressing. In much the same way that the slowing down in the rate of economic growth prompted interest in planning methods during the early and mid-1960s, attention is once again being given to the longer-term growth prospects of the economy. This is reflected in some restoration of prestige for the National Economic Development Council and in the current Labour government's commitment to planning agreements with the country's largest companies.

The recent depreciation of sterling from its 1972 level and the negotiations for international credit, although in part a short-term expedient, are also part of a further long-term effort to reduce the external burdens on the domestic economy. The reductions in real living standards and the substantial increase in the unemployment rate consequent upon negative growth rates in 1974 and 1975 have forced economists and the authorities alike into undertaking a fundamental review of the longer-term consequences of the cycle of short-term policy adjustment, and of the balance between manufacturing and a wide range of public sector activities. There does in fact appear to be some political commitment to giving greater priority to manufacturing activities and investment in it, as a means of taking advantage of sterling's depreciation to achieve an export-led reversal of the growth-trend.

Few commentators and certainly not the authors of this case study would see this redress of balance as a panacea solution. The case study tried to refer to a wide range of critical influences. The overview section on supply-side factors important to growth rate analysis is intended to act as a basis for further discussion – the nature of the input/output relationship may be illuminated by reference to further international comparison or to a less aggregated picture. It is important to bear in mind that economic growth: '. . . is the manifestation at the aggregate level of all changes in factor inputs and efficiency at the level of the firm or establishment'.[4] The input-output approach however stresses the supply-side of the economy, whereas traditional, static macroeconomics emphasizes the income-expenditure relationship. The authors were particularly concerned with the dynamic inter-relationship between aggregate demand and supply – an element which short-term demand management inevitably overlooks. Even macrodynamic theory, although starting from the dual role of investment (namely its income- and capacity-generating effects) tends to concentrate on the conditions required to keep income and output growing in equilibrium, rather than on the ways in which changes or fluctuations in aggregate demand influence the growth of output. The political nature of the adjustment process in any case encouraged the authorities to opt for short-term tinkering with the economy rather than for consistent medium and longer-term strategies.[5]

The form of government economic management and the role and size of the public sector are clearly politically, emotive topics. But there are also important issues involved in terms of the nature and fluctuations of public expenditure and public sector activities, and of the problems of valuing many public sector activities within the existing national accounting framework.

REFERENCES

1. *The Economic Implications of Full Employment*, Cmnd. 9725, HMSO, March 1956, p. 10.
2. NEDC, *Growth of the UK Economy to 1966*, London, HMSO 1963, p. vii.
3. *See*, for example, A Maddison, *Economic Growth in the West*, Allen & Unwin, 1964.
4. A. Whiting, 'An International Comparison of the Instability of Economic Growth', *Three Banks Review*, March 1976, p. 26.
5. R. W. Bacon and W. A. Eltis, 'Stop-Go and De-industrialisation', *National Westminster Bank Review*, November 1975, pp. 31–44.

FURTHER READING

ON THE WEST GERMANY ECONOMY

R. G. Opie, 'Western Germany's economic miracle', *Three Banks Review*, 1962, pp. 3–17.
'The German lesson', Survey in *The Economist*, 15 October 1966.
'A time to ask questions', Survey in *The Economist*, 1 December 1973.

ON THE UNITED KINGDOM ECONOMY

R. Bacon and W. Eltis, *Britain's Economic problem: too few producers*, MacMillan, 1976.

S. Brittan, *Steering The Economy*, Pelican, 1971.

R. Caves (ed.), *Britain's Economic Prospects*, Allen & Unwin, 1968.

F. W. Paish, 'Business cycles in Britain', *Lloyds Bank Review*, October 1970, pp. 1–22.

'Economics: New Oxford', Business Brief in *The Economist*, 29 November, 1975, pp. 76–77.

In particular attention is drawn to National Economic Development Office, *Cyclical Fluctuations in the United Kingdom Economy*, Discussion Paper, 1976.

POINTS INTENDED TO BE RAISED FROM THE QUESTIONS

1. It should be recognized that economic growth requires an increase in the *real* value of output, not in the monetary value. High inflation rates and consequently high rates of growth in money income disguise the fact that 'physical' output has not increased rapidly in the UK.

2. There are two major reasons why the standard of living might be falling as RGNP is increasing. The rate of population growth might exceed the rate of growth of real output and therefore per capita income will be declining. However, even if per capita income is increasing, the distribution of the Real Gross National Product may be changing in such a way that it lowers the 'average' standard of living in the economy.

3. Industrialization involves a transfer of labour from agricultural to industrial employment. In a less advanced economy there exist greater opportunities for transfers of this kind, since a higher proportion of labour is still employed in the agricultural sector. Growth potential benefits as a consequence because productivity in agriculture is invariably much lower than labour productivity in industrial employment in the less advanced economy.

4. Three causes are stressed in this study:

   1. The redistribution of labour between industries – in particular the movement from the agricultural sector to the manufacturing sector;
   2. The employment of a larger volume of capital goods with a given labour force may lead to higher productivity;
   3. Technological progress can bring improvement in the quality of capital goods making the combination of labour and capital inputs more productive.

5. The main point which this question intends to raise is the synchronization which results from the expansion of trade among member states, that is the increasing interdependence of member states. An expansion of output and income in one member state is transmitted to other member states through an increase in imports from other member states (the marginal propensity to import is high).

One would hope that economic harmonization and co-ordination of policies within the EEC would also, if not eliminate fluctuations completely, minimize them and again lead to a synchronization of the cycle among the member states.

6. That governments are responsible for stabilizing the economy implies that economic systems are subject to erratic shocks or endogenous cyclical forces, shocks such as the rise in oil prices or the discovery of North Sea oil, and cyclical forces generated possibly by the adjustment or replacement of the capital stock. The text also makes reference to the international transmission of cycles.

The elimination or reduction of fluctuations requires efficient forecasting techniques in order that the direction, amplitude and timing of counter-cyclical policies may be effective. Destabilizing policies may occur therefore because of data deficiencies and inadequate models of the economy, or because governments are unable or unwilling to adopt optimal policies. The timing of general elections may for instance influence the 'stop/go' pattern of development. Alternatively conflicting policy targets may make the avoidance of fluctuations difficult, especially where the authorities are reluctant to use sufficient policy instruments.

7. Fluctuation has several features – amplitude, frequency, and time structure. For measurement of the amplitude of fluctuation, it is possible that the average growth may not be the appropriate target to adopt if for instance it involves consistent under-utilization of resources or divergence from other policy targets. Some investigations have concentrated on potential, full employment or balanced growth targets.

In addition the use of annual RGNP figures may obscure variations on a monthly or quarterly basis, or fluctuations at a less aggregated level of the economy. The authors are in particular concerned with the pattern of fluctuation of the categories of expenditure, and with the movement of domestic spending or absorption in relation to output.

8. It is important to view expenditure not only as the way in which income is used but also as the manner in which output is absorbed. Hence in the UK during the post-war period, boom years have been typified by the overshooting of output by domestic spending, with the result that imports grew rapidly and potential exports were diverted to the home market. The authorities' attempts to improve the balance

of payments problems usually in the form of deflationary policies, tended to reduce the growth of investment spending particularly severely. There is of course some danger in interpreting this conflict between investment and export growth as a causal factor of the UK's slower growth rates, when it may in fact be an effect of slower growth.

9. It is tempting to interpret West Germany's significantly higher investment ratio as the explanation of the growth differential in labour productivity. Clearly the growth of the capital/labour ratio is an important variable, not least because it is likely to influence the rate of technical progress through the greater opportunities for embodying new ideas and for experience of new methods. However, it is also important to emphasize other than the quantitative aspects of capital accumulation – namely the quality, direction and utilization of capital.

10. The text concentrates on the impact of government stabilization policies on labour mobility and the distribution of labour between sectors. It would be possible also to consider the impact of a whole range of regional and industrial policies on factor mobility in general, and on attitudes and labour market power. The authors however emphasize the impact of full employment policies on various aspects of labour mobility, e.g. between skills. They suggest that bottlenecks and the lead of wages over productivity have contributed directly to the inflationary spiral and loss of competitiveness of UK goods during the 1960s. In addition they examine the role of public sector employment as a buffer against fluctuations in manufacturing employment. The longer-term effects on manufacturings' share of the labour force and therefore on growth potential are clearly brought out in Table 5.5.

The possibility that the authors have identified an effect rather than a cause of slower economic growth remains. Similarly it is also important to avoid labelling public sector activities as 'non-productive'.